EYES
OF A
Man

LESTER WITCHER JR.

Copyright © 2023 Lester Witcher Jr.

All rights reserved. No part of this book may be reproduced, stored, or transmitted by any means—whether auditory, graphic, mechanical, or electronic—without written permission of both publisher and author, except in the case of brief excerpts used in critical articles and reviews. Unauthorized reproduction of any part of this work is illegal and is punishable by law.

ISBN: 979-8-88640-857-7 (sc)
ISBN: 979-8-88640-858-4 (hc)
ISBN: 979-8-88640-859-1 (e)

Because of the dynamic nature of the Internet, any web addresses or links contained in this book may have changed since publication and may no longer be valid. The views expressed in this work are solely those of the author and do not necessarily reflect the views of the publisher, and the publisher hereby disclaims any responsibility for them.

One Galleria Blvd., Suite 1900, Metairie, LA 70001
1-888-421-2397

Contents

Action 1
All I Need 2
Always By Our Side 3
April Showers 4
As The Days Go By 6
As the Pain in My Heart Grows 8
At Ease 9
Birthday Wish 10
Bitter Sweet 11
Breaking Point 13
Brown Eyes 14
Cabin Fever 15
Change 18
Christmas Wish 20
Colorful Eyes 22
Come Home Girl 24
Complicated 26
Cover Girl 28
Crazy in Love 30
Dark 31
Darkness Falls 33
Disappointment 35
Divine Surrender 36
Don't Forget Me 37
Don't Run Away 39
Easily Be Broken 41
Extra Special 44
Eyes of a Man 46
Faithful 52
Feelings 56

Find Love	58
Fire Place	60
Ghost Left in My Heart	63
Give My All	65
Golden Girl	66
Good to the Last Drop	68
Grandmother	71
Green Eyes	74
Happy Valentine's Day	76
Harvest Moon	77
Heaven Sent	81
Heavens Above	84
Honest	86
Hot Tonight	87
I Love You	92
I Miss U!	94
I Want To Be Naughty, Do You?	96
I Will Not Give Up On You	99
If You Need Me	100
I'm Sorry!	102
J.A.M.I.E.	103
JC Crazy	105
Keep Sake	107
Ladylove	109
Let Go	110
Lollipop	112
Lonely Heart	114
Lose Control	115
Lost In Feelings	117
Love and Hate	119
Love Is Not For Me	121
Love You and Hold On	122
Luscious Beauty	124
Luv	131
M.P.D. (Most Precious Desire)	132

Midnight Love	134
Mind, Body & Soul	137
Mine	138
Mother	141
Mutual Love	144
My Blue Moon Turns To Gold	146
My Heart Cries Out!	147
My Heart Desires	149
My Soul Is Calling Out To You!	151
Night Unfolds	153
On Our Side	157
Once In A Lifetime	159
Out of Control	161
Out of my Life	164
Passionate Kiss	165
Past Love	167
Prayer for Grandma	169
Precious Moment	171
Pretty in Pink	173
Rain	175
Raindrops Fall	176
S.W.C. (Sexy White Chocolate)	177
Scared	178
The Scent of a Woman	180
Second to None	182
Sexy & Sweet	183
Sexy Lover	185
Sexy, Kind & Unforgettable	186
Shoulder To Lean On!	188
Silent Wish	190
Snuggle Blanket	192
Special	194
Stolen Moments	196
Stormy Weather	198
Sweet Prince	200

Tasty Love	202
Time For Love Is Up!	203
True Friend	206
Uncertain	208
Void in My Heart	209
Walk Away	211
Warmed My Soul	213
When Our Eyes Met	215
Within Your Hearts	216
Work Family	217
Yearn For You	218

Action

Life is like a maze
If you don't be careful
You can become lost
In a world of aches & pains
So when you feel down & out
Just remember you are not alone
So take a deep breathe
And concentrate on a solution
To take you away from it all
But no matter what the outcome
Stay focused & relaxed
Therefore, you can master the problems
Left by the maze
As you, take Action!

Actions speaks louder than words
However, it also helps to talk
To your partner in a relationship
So he or she knows how
One another feels inside
Because if you make that mistake
And let it go on without
The communication
It can lead to disaster
And very easily corrupt your mind
While you sit and let a good thing end
As you fail to take Action!

All I Need

Baby I want you all day
Just so, I can love you
Please tell me you will stay
And let us cherish the moment
Just for another day
That is all I need

All I need is you to love me right
Chase away my fears during the night
Keep me safe and warm
And someday you will know
What it means to be
All I need

Baby I want you more
Then you could ever know
Let me lay you down
And rub your body slow
Keep your heart with me
Then you will see
What you mean to me
That is all I need

Always By Our Side

My life is in a dark cloud
And I am losing myself to this pain
However, I do not know where or when it will end
Because I just want to throw in the towel
And to stop being a burden to everyone
So I think of just ending it all
Then all of a sudden, you come into my life
When I thought my life was at a dead-end
You brought me hope and support
To see the light at the end of the tunnel
And things can get better if you believe
Because God is always by our side

You took me by my hand and said a prayer for me
As you finished you said it would be ok
Because the man upstairs will never let you down
As long as you put faith in him always
He will lead you as his son down the right path
As they say, he places people in your life
For special reasons and at the right time
And it was you to help me through this pain
Because he speaks to us in different ways
While he watches over us always in spirit
Because God is always by our side

April Showers

As I walk over to the window
And pull back the curtains
I look out over the April sky
And I see the dark clouds passing by
As it begins to lightly rain outside
And I crack the windows open
As the cool breeze blows upon my face
Because it is the start of the April Showers

As a steady rain begins to fall
I go and pull up a chair next to the window
As I begin to watch the raindrops
And at that same moment outside
I hear voices and laughter
As the sound moves closer to my window
I stand up to see what is going on
And it is a couple dancing in the rain
As they enjoy the April Showers

As I stare and watch the couple dance in the rain
A warm feeling came over me
As the couple holds each other, close
He begins to wipe away the rain from her face
While she begins to smile from ear to ear
As he swoops her off her feet
And spins her around in the air
As the rain drips from their clothes
Outside as they play in the April Showers

The rain begins to come down heavier outside
Nevertheless, that does not stop them from dancing
As cars slow down to watch as they pass by
It just makes them dance more & more
As they wave to those that, pass them by
The joy they have from it shows on their faces
Because true love like this is hard to find
But this is what happens during April Showers

As The Days Go By

When I am with you, I feel safe
Because your presence drives me wild
And the sweet smell of your perfume
Produces goose bumps all over my body
As I try to shake the sensation
Because my feelings for you
Burns so deep inside my soul
You are all I can think about
As the days, go by

Let us take a trip to the beach
Therefore, we can walk along the sand
As the moonlight is bright
While I hold you tight
And keep you warm through the night
As I gaze into your eyes
And pull you oh so close
So I can give you a big kiss
And place the blanket down
As I start to massage your shoulders
Because you're all I think about
As the days, go by

*Sitting alone at night makes me sad
But when I close my eyes
And start to picture your lovely smile
It turns my sadness to gold
Because the time we spend together
Is so special to me
Because you're all I think about
As the days, go by*

*We need to talk seriously for a moment
Because there is a lot, I want to say
However, I do not want to scare you off
Because what I feel for you is real
And if we explain our feelings to one another
We might both be able to take the next step
And commit ourselves to our destiny
Because you're all I think about
As the days, go by*

As the Pain in My Heart Grows

Winter has come early
And my dreams are dashed
By the letter that I'm reading
Saying that we need time apart
So you can find your love for me again
But knowing that your love has faded
And our lives together maybe over
As the pain in my heart grows

I sit by the phone waiting for you to call
As I stare at the walls
With tears running down my face
And imagining where we went wrong
However, all I can picture is you in my mind
With you standing there inside my arms
As I hold you close to my soul
And knowing your not coming home
As the pain in my heart grows

As I lay my head on the pillow
And cry myself to sleep
I begin to dream of you my dear
As I see that lovely smile of yours
That makes me lose my mind
And sends a chill down my spine
Just as I go to kiss you in my dream
The alarm goes off and I wake up
Looking around hoping that you're standing there
Nevertheless, my wish did not come true
As the pain in my heart grows

At Ease

How do I keep falling in love?
With someone, that does not feel the same way
In addition, I just cannot escape this pain
That I continue to run into over & over
Maybe one day these feeling will go away
Nevertheless, until then I need to find serenity
For my heart to be at ease

One plus one equals two but you just want to be one
And I want to do anything and everything to be with you
Nevertheless, you just want to be friends with benefits
And want me all to yourself
However, you do not want anyone else to have me
This concept I just do not understand
Especially when you have feelings for me
And you are not willing to commit to me
As we go day by day with these feelings
I need to find a point to breakaway
Therefore, my heart can be at ease

I do not want to give up on you
Because there is something special, I see in you
But I also do not want to miss happiness
And someone that will commit to be with me
Because I'm not getting any younger
And I just want to be happily in love
Therefore, I can spend my life with that someone
And not have to worry about anything in life
Except to make them happy
From morning to night and anytime leftover
Therefore, my heart can be at ease

Birthday Wish

Today is your day that God made for you
In addition, I hope it is everything that you wish it would be
Because you deserve to enjoy this special day
And I am just sending you this wish from my heart
Just to let you know Happy Birthday from me
And to let you know you are thought of each & everyday
Even without it being this special day
I am at a loss for words
Therefore, I am going to end this with this Birthday Wish!

I am sending you many blessings to enjoy this wonderful day
And be successful in everything you do
Because life can be confusing
And you have a very bright future ahead of you
I wish you the best Birthday Wish!

Bitter Sweet

From the first time our eyes met
I knew that you were the one
With each and every passing moment
I cannot deny my feelings are so true
Because you are the blessing
That I have prayed for to be in my life
And God has granted me you
Because he understands what we have been through
In our past and what we need for our future
And he has sent me to you and you to me
Because of what I feel deep inside my soul
It's Bitter Sweet

Life has many obstacles to over come
But in this short time period
I realized that you captured my soul
And the only thing I want
Is to make you a part of my life
With my gentle touch
And your strong arms around me
As I caress you from head to toe
Because these feeling for you
Are Bitter Sweet

Time and time again my body quivers for you
My soul has witnessed the beauty
Of what it feels to be in love again
And now that these feelings got me floating in the clouds
I can't imagine what I feel will ever end
Because you & God have given a fresh start on life
And it has been a wonderful experience for me
But I just want to ride these feelings
Until I reach the finish line with you
As we walk hand in hand & arm and arm
Because these feelings I have for you
Are Bitter Sweet

Breaking Point

Why is love so hard to find
It keeps tearing me apart
Just when I am feeling love
I seem to run into heartache
And the pain is heavy on my soul
While my eyes, begin to tear
As I reach my breaking point

Life has great hills to climb
And being in love has a price
Because each time I feel love
I get my heart torn apart
And I fade into the dark
Because I attract the wrong kind
And it is hard to stay positive
As I reach my breaking point

I do not think love is for me
Because every time I receive heartache
And it hurts me deep inside
However, I continue to pray for love
And wish for that special someone
To come into my life
And bring me much joy & happiness
Because my heart is crying out loud
To be free from all this pain
As I reach my breaking point

Brown Eyes

Standing in the distance watching you
As the camera's flash constantly
And you strike pose after pose
As you stare at me and I smile at you
Because you can't wait to finish
The successful photo shoot
To go celebrate over dinner
And sip on some wine by candle light
As I place your hand inside of mine
And the light shines upon your brown eyes

As the candles burn under the moonlight
And the violin player plays a romantic tune
As we get up to slow dance
To allow our bodies to intertwine
As the sweet smell of your perfume
Causes me to caress you deep in my arms
And the gentle stroke of your fingertips
Move up and down my spine
As my blood, pressure starts to rise
And the light shines upon your brown eyes

The table is set and our dinner is ready
As I escort you to your chair
And pull it out and hold your hand
As I gently place you in your seat
And kiss the top of your hand
As I move toward my chair
And sit down in front of you
As I lick my lips to blow you a kiss
And the look on your face is priceless
As the light shines upon your brown eyes

Cabin Fever

My busy workweek has just ended
And it is time to head to the Poconos
Because this is, the guys weekend away
And we are going to kick it at the resort
Maybe do some skiing and tubing
And maybe just hang out at the bar
As we have some drinks and site see
But first things first is to arrive safely
As I go home and gather my things
I call the entire party on the phone
And make sure we are almost ready
To get to our destination in the Poconos
And be ready to catch some Cabin Fever

As we arrive at the resort to check in
I look toward the office window
And I cannot believe what I am seeing
Because I see the loveliest woman in my life
As I tell the guys to hurry up
Therefore, I can get a closer look at her
But as I rush in to cross her path
Just as I enter the office, she is gone
However, I cannot wait to see her again
Because her radiant beauty has blown my mind
And I have a case of Cabin Fever

As we get our keys to our cabin rooms
I fade into a daze just picturing her face
And as my friends are shouting my name
I snap out of it and head into my room
However, as I get settle in with my things
All I can think about is her beauty
And all I want to do is to find out her name
Because I am hoping, I get to meet her
And put a name to her lovely face
As it keeps running over & over in my mind
Because after seeing her this weekend
Has caused me to have Cabin Fever

I have not run into her at all the whole trip
Nevertheless, I am still looking for her lovely smile
And all I want to do is to run into her again
But it is now our last day here at the resort
And it is time to check out and return home
Because I am feeling lonely deep inside
I begin to load my things into the van
And I get a page to come to the front desk
As I head down the hall to get my page
I pass by a cute couple-walking arm in arm
And I hope to be like that someday soon
As I reach the desk, I get a tap on the back
And it is you standing there pretty as can be
As you finally got the nerve to speak to me
Because you had a case of Cabin Fever

Change

What have I done?
To be pushed away from you
I just cannot go on
With my head in the clouds
I need some time to myself
To dig deep down inside
And see if I need this pain
That's tearing me apart inside
Relying on my dreams
Is hurting me even more
Therefore, I am taking this time
To make a change

The support you gave me
Was ooh so sweet?
The times we shared
Made my love grow skin deep
Because of you I thought
I had the world
You crushed my heart
With your lack of respect
I had to move on
With my dignity and pride
And I clearly made a change

Walking along the shore
With the moon shining bright
Upon my face
I wished upon a star
And gazed across the ocean
With the cool spring breeze
Blowing on my skin
Sitting on the sand
Counting my blessings in my heart
That has come and gone
It brings on a change

With weeks gone by
And my mind is clear
I am able to face
The world with a new attitude
My problems are behind me
And the fellas & I are together again
Out having a good time
And staying out of trouble
I am glad I went through
This painful feeling inside
Because of you girl
I made that important change

Christmas Wish

My life has been less than average
And it gets me down this time of year
Because I never seem to catch a break
And just when it seems to be getting better
My luck turns and something else goes wrong
But as I sit here and think about my life
And ask myself repeatedly
Will this be my year for change?
As I pray for a special Christmas Wish

I have good days and bad days
But I never show what's going on inside
Because I like to keep my thoughts private
And I do not need anyone feeling sorry for me
Because times are hard enough
And my life is complicated on its own
As this time of year comes around
I only pray for a Christmas Wish

Someday I hope that I can catch a break
And get my life above average
Therefore, I can provide my love with the world
Because I know, she deserves better
And I think she loves me anyway
Nevertheless, all I want to do is make her happy
And to give her the life of a queen
Because that means I have receive my Christmas Wish

Colorful Eyes

It's Friday and I am heading to the club
To hang out with friends
And to have a good time blowing off steam
As we arrive at the club
I cannot wait to get my groove on
And try to find that special woman
However, normally I never have such luck
As we walk inside, I scan the place
To see if anyone catches my eye
As I head towards the bar
Nevertheless, I am looking for that lovely woman
With those sexy colorful eyes

As the night goes on, I start to get discouraged
And it seems that the night is wasted
But as soon as I turn toward the door
I see you standing there all alone
And your radiant beauty freezes the room
As my heart skips a beat
And I head in your direction
To introduce myself and ask your name
Then you turn and make eye contact
As you stare with those sexy colorful eyes

I ask your name and you say Jaime
As the soft sound of your voice
Sends goose bumps up & down my spine
The scent of your perfume captures my soul
As I ask you to dance to my song
You are hesitant to respond
Nevertheless, your girl tells you to go ahead

And then you say let's go
As we reach the dance floor
You take my hand and we start to dance
As we hold each other, close
I look down at you as you pull your hair back
And I cannot help but to stare at you
Because of those sexy colorful eyes

As the song ends, we start back to the bar
And your girl takes you to the ladies room
Because she is curious to see what you think
About me and if you're interested in me
However, all you could do is smile
And you told her maybe let's see
He is handsome and he approached me
And he seems like he is genuinely sweet
However, you want to learn more
And you start back to the bar
As you, make your way through the crowd
Our eyes connect once again
And all I can do is just shake my head
Because of those sexy colorful eyes

Come Home Girl

No one likes to be alone in the dark
However, when pain strikes the heart
And the tears begin to fall
Because of what is going on in your soul
It just seems to be unbearable
And you wish that it all would end
However, the pain deepens inside
And all that I wish to come true
Is that you come home girl

I sit here with tears in my eyes
Just thinking of what I have done
To drive you away from me
And the pain your feeling inside
I want you to know that sorry
Will never change the pain in your heart
However, I will spend a lifetime
Making it up to you my dear
All I am wishing for now
Is that you come home girl

I try to reach you on the phone
But you refuse to return my calls
And I send you flowers and things
But you just send them right back
And I can tell that you are hurting inside
As you, continue to ignore me
Please baby I want you here

Therefore, we can resolve the pain I have caused
And that we can start over from scratch
Because I love you deeply
And I am wishing upon a star
That you please come home girl

As the sun begins to shine on the windowpane
And I realize that I have been up all night
Just praying that you will come home
And we can work on this love
We once shared for one another
And that you can forgive me
Because I realize that, I am not complete
Unless you're in my heart and soul
As I drop to my knees and pray to God
That you please come home girl

Complicated

I cannot turn off these feelings
That you cause me
Because it's a special attraction
And it grows inside me
When I am near you
Day by day
And week to week
But I cannot react
On my thoughts
Because our lives
Are complicated

I bring the best out of you
And it makes you hot
But it clouds your mind
Because we both know the risk
That it would cause
Even though it could be astonishing
And enjoyable for us
We realize its best
That we keep it cool
Because our attraction
Is complicated

I picture you from head to toe
With me rubbing, you up & down
Making you hotter & hotter
And removing your clothes
One garment at a time
And have you close your eyes

While you imagine what is next
As you start to sweat
And bite your lip
But wanting more
As the attraction grows
Just knowing the situation
Makes things complicated

Your loyalty is with your spouse
But your temptation is strong
And it drives you wild
Because you would love a taste
But it could lead to more
And if acted upon
It could present feelings
That might change everything
And the attraction grows
Into a soulful passion
But also provides
Many questions
To be answered
And it could change lives
As the attraction grows
Just knowing the stakes
Of the matter
Makes it complicated

Cover Girl

When I watch, you walk
And think about you
I get a warm feeling inside
Just hoping to be noticed
By your lovely blue eyes
Therefore, I can describe you from head to toe
Because you're my Cover Girl

Being a true blonde is a plus
Because it suits your face
While your soft lips
Gives me the chills up & down my spine
And your silky smooth skin
Drives me wild with every touch
And your body structure is perfect
To hold you oh so tight
As I melt like butter
While I slide down your sexy legs
And massage your lovely feet
Because you're my Cover Girl

I want to be naughty do you?
Being nice is my pride & joy
But every once in awhile
You have to let your guard down
To be able to experience both sides
And take many chances
I would like to take that risk
With you for awhile
Because you're my Cover Girl

As the days, go by
I cannot get you off my mind
Because your beauty
Lures me closer to you
I cannot fight this feeling
Because I just can't hide it anymore
I want to run my fingers through your hair
And give you a sample of what is in store
As I go down and suck on your toes
As you let me know, how it feels
While I keep my hands to myself
And let the time pass us by
If you want me to stop
Just say the word
However, I guarantee you will enjoy yourself
While I stroke each & every toe
With my sensational touch
Because you're my Cover Girl

Crazy in Love

Standing along the sandy shore
As the cool summer breeze blows by
And the smell of the water is in the air
As I stare out upon the ocean light
Just as I begin to walk the shore
I stop along the rocks to sit down
And I begin to toss stones into the water
As I think of my life's journey
Because I am missing my baby
And it hurts to be apart from her
Because I'm crazy in love

As the waves crash upon the shore
While my heart feels lost
Because I'm missing my baby
I can picture her pretty smile
And the scent of her perfume
As I see that sexy sparkle in her eyes
Because she means the world to me
And in a few more days
I can hold her in my arms
And never let her go
Because I'm crazy in love

Dark

All my life I gave my heart
But it just seems hopeless
All I want is to be happy
But my luck is bad
And all I get is heartaches
Just praying for love
In a way I should be loved
But life is a coin toss
You can be either happy or sad
But everyone wants to be happy
And be worry free
But trying for the best
Can leave you with a smile
While you count your blessings
Or with a frown
As you fade into the dark!

To be lost in love
Is a painful situation to overcome
When you are all alone
And on your last leg
Because without any support
Your mind becomes frantic
While your heart pays the price
As you try to stay afloat
And try to avoid fading
Into the dark!

Day by day, you hold onto dreams
But you cannot hide the pain
And the heartaches
That is tearing you apart
All I do is feel the discomfort
In the trials & tribulations in my life
All I am trying to do is be careful
With the decisions I make in judgment
And find the light
That will lead me out of the dark!

Darkness Falls

I cannot explain my thoughts about you
Because I had you running through my mind
And I could not shake the thoughts of you
Because my heart kept calling your name
And my body needed your gentle touch
As I begin to close my eyes, I pictured you
Standing in front of me looking sad
As you began to hold out your arms
And walk slowly toward me in distress
I hurry up to hold you tight in my arms
And let you know I am here for you
Because I want you to feel safe
While your deep inside my arms
As the darkness falls

As I can feel your heartbeat along with mine
I can only imagine what you are going through
However, I want you to calm down before we speak
Because I want to be at my best for you
As you open up your heart to me
Because I feel our hearts beating as one
As you, squeeze me tighter in your arms
And I know you can count on me
As you, begin to shed tears upon my chest
Because of the sadness brought to your soul
As the darkness falls

I begin to escort you toward the house
As I wipe away the tears on your face
And whisper in your ear that you are safe
Because you will have no more worries
As long as you are inside my arms
And that I will warm you from head to toe
However, that still will not bring back the joy inside
Because your faith in men are torn to shreds
And I know that only time will tell you the truth
Because as long as the pain is inside your heart
No matter what I say or do, it will be an afterthought
Because of the bad feeling that were left behind
As the darkness falls

You are trembling from head to toe with fear
And I do not know what to do with you
Nevertheless, all I can think of is to calm you down
Because until you can let me help you
I will just be another person out to hurt you
And I promise you that I am here to help
Because as I see you are hurting, I am hurting
And that just breaks my heart knowing you are in pain
Nevertheless, I will not rush you into trusting me at all
Because when that time comes, I will be ready
As you call upon me to touch your soul
Because I have feeling for you, I cannot explain
However, as you told me once before that you missed me
And from that moment I kept thinking of you
Because those words unlocked something inside
And all I see in my dreams every night is you
As the darkness falls

Disappointment

I am sitting here reflecting on my life
And I cannot explain what I am feeling
Because I feel that I let you down
And I just want to isolate myself
From the world, family and friends
Because I have been a disgrace
And I have let you down heavenly father
Because you gave your life for me
And I have been nothing but a Disappointment

Heavenly father forgive me for my ignorance
And not being the son that you made me to be
Because I know I could have done better
And made you proud of me
Nevertheless, I wasted my time and the opportunity
You have allowed me to have in your presence
However, what I did was not held up on my end
And was nothing but a Disappointment

I know that you always forgive your children
Nevertheless, I cannot even begin to forgive myself
So until I can find that forgiveness
I will never feel worthy to be your son
Because until I can forgive myself
I will always be a Disappointment

Divine Surrender

Staring across the boardwalk upon the stars
I hear a sensual voice blow through the wind
And as I turn, I see this glowing smile
Attached to this oh so tantalizing body
Perched above the parking lot hill top
And all I could see is the twinkle in her eyes
Wanting to fall into Divine Surrender

As I slowly make my way toward her
My heart starts to beat out of turn
And I feel my knees start to shake
While my tongue twists in knots as, I speak
And I cannot gather my thoughts to ask her name
Because my palms are sweaty and cold
And I try not to fall into Divine Surrender

I finally make it to her up close
And she reaches out and touches my skin
As I begin to breakout into a sweat
She tells me her name as I try to gather myself
I clear my throat and say my name
As I focus on my thoughts
I cannot escape her beauty
As I fall deeper into Divine Surrender

Don't Forget Me

There comes a time
When times are sad
And tears are shed
Overall, you are loved
I cannot find the words
To say how much you are missed
All I can say is do not forget me!

As long as you breathe
And walk on this earth
I will always be there for you
Through rain and snow
Alternatively, whatever the case may be
Because as I write this you're missed
Now that you're leaving
Just listen to what I'm about to say
The special place in my heart for you
I will lock-up and give you the key
And protect that place with my life
Because you're so special to me
And I pray you do not forget me!

Even though we cannot hang out
I will treasure those memories
That we spent laughing & talking
Because I wish you the best
And you will always be my cover girl
No matter what the cost
Because I care
More than you know
And trust me
You are always on my mind
So please do not forget me!

As I wipe the tears from my face
I will take this time to pray
And hope to hang out again
But if not take care of yourself
And enjoy your life
Because you're missed deeply
And as I close the chapter
Just remember only you can unlock
That special place in my heart
Because you hold the key
So whatever happens?
Please do not forget me!

Don't Run Away

I enjoy our conversations
Even though you run away
When your feelings
Come into question
However, that is good
Because you have feelings
That you are scared to show how you feel
Because you're so confused
That is ok
But in order to be loved
Open up your heart slowly
Nevertheless, don't run away

You have feelings for me
But can't express them
Because your fear is great
And you do not want to be hurt
But you are safe
Because I care for you deeply
And want to give you the world
Because words can't explain
What my heart feels for you
That is no lie
Because you're loved
But don't run away

The words I speak to you
About how I feel
Makes you think at times
About what you are missing
Or passing up on
And if I'm truly sincere
When I tell you how I feel
I understand totally
However, you are all I think about
Because you're special to me
And I have never felt
This way before
And it drives me wild
Over and over for you
So please don't run away

Your kisses make me melt
While your touch
Sends chills down my spine
But the only thing
I can picture
Is me being with you
And you wanting to be loved
Just like, you imagined
So please don't run away

Easily Be Broken

I just cannot believe
I have been such a fool
To trust you with my feelings
Because I did everything, I could
To tell myself it is not true
But all I was doing was holding on
To something, that was an illusion
And realizing that it was fake
By destroying my confidence
I once had for you
And my friends warned me
But I was deep in love
To even listen and see reality
Now I know that if you fall in love
Do not give your heart
Because it can easily be broken!

I thought we had it all
And I couldn't ask for anything more
Than the love I possessed inside of me
For you and only you
But you shattered my heart
With your selfishness towards me
I hope you are satisfied and proud
For the pain you have caused
In my heart with your actions
I wish someday you'd get to encounter
How a heart can easily be broken!

But I cannot dwell on the past
I have to look at my future
And what it might hold
But as far as I'm concerned
You have taught me a lot
And even though I am in pain
I would like to thank you
For opening my eyes
And showing me
That you should never play
With anyone's heart
Because it can easily be broken!

Now three months have passed
And I am doing just fine
Without you in my life
Because I'm starting over
As I see, you are not doing well
You start calling me again
And you tell me
You made a huge mistake
But I cannot take you back
Because I refuse to be drawn in
And go through it all over again
All I can think about
Is how you treated me?
And now you know
How a heart can easily be broken!

While you see the consequences
Of being alone and in pain
You might consider being faithful
In your next romance
And try to keep that person
Who loves you with his heart?
And you may not have to ever
Feel how a heart can easily be broken!

Extra Special

I cannot believe it is so late and cold
As I flag down a taxi to get home
I begin to feel raindrops upon my face
And as the cab pulls up it begins to rain
However, I get in just in time to keep dry
As I watch, the raindrops through the window
And the Vegas lights continue to shine bright
I begin to think of fond memories of her
And what she meant to me in my life
As a smile creeps up upon my face
I cannot help but to think of her
And how she made me feel deep inside
As I hold on to our great times, we shared
Because she made me feel extra special

I am out here in Vegas trying to cope
Because losing you left a big void in my heart
And no matter how many times I cry
It will not bring you back to me
And I wish there was something I could do
However, I am trying not to lose my mind
And it is hard when you lose someone so special
Because you were my perfect soul mate
And god allowed me to have the cream of the crop
Because you made me feel extra special

As the days, get longer without you
And I use this away time to think of you
Nevertheless, with each step it gets tougher
And as I pass couples on the Vegas strip
I remember how we walked side by side
And how people use to stop and stare at us
As we walked by arm and arm
Hugging, kissing and holding each other close
However, all of my dreams have ended
Because you are gone from my life
Nevertheless, you will always have my heart
Because you made me feel extra special

As I pull, back the curtains of my room
And watch the sunset out over the horizon
Because I finally have come to peace
With you not being here in my life
And how much I miss holding you close
As I kneel down to pray to our father
And let him know that you are in a better place
Because he has, you right by his side
And will always let you smile upon me
Because he has set you, free from all pain
And I thank him for given you peace
Nevertheless, I will always love you so much
Because you made me feel extra special

Eyes of a Man

As the sunrises over the horizon
The bright light shines upon my face
As I reach to close the blinds
I get a glace of this lovely creature
Jogging along the sand
As the stiff summer breeze blows against her face
I fall deep into a trance as I watch her go by
With the sun shining on her beautiful skin
And the seagulls flying high above
As she stops to stare across the ocean
And I just cannot explain what I see
Looking through the eyes of a man

She begins to stretch before she continue her run
As she looks toward the house
She sees me standing in the bedroom window
And she waves at me to say hello neighbor
I almost go into shock at the blink of an eye
And she begins to jog back to her place
Along the sand as the water runs across her feet
As I follow her to the front door
And she washes off the sand upon her legs
As I take a deep breath and step outside
To get a glance of her from head to toe
Before she steps inside and closes the door
As I imagine her standing there in front of me
Looking through the eyes of a man

As the afternoon hour approaches
I hear a knock at the door
And as I open, the door standing there it is she
I just get goose bumps seeing her so close
And I cannot speak a word at first
Nevertheless, I gather myself to say hello
As she, introduces herself as Cindy
I tell her my name and invite her in
Because it's the right thing to do
And she asks me if she is interrupting something
As I clear my throat and say no
I ask her to have a seat
And if she would like a drink
However, she says she wanted to meet me
After seeing me this morning in the window
And wanted to meet her new neighbor
As she welcomed me to the area
Looking through the eyes of a man

As she is walking away, she turns
And invites me to her swimsuit party later on
However, I am hesitant but I say yes
As she says, I will see you then
I just start grinning from ear to ear
With joy and excitement upon my face
And run upstairs to go through my swim trunks
As I lay them out on the bed
I run across a new pair never worn
And they are perfect for attending her party
To make an impression on her and her friends
As I meet them for the first time
Looking through the eyes of a man

As I get ready for the party my phone rings
And it is my cousin and he is stopping by
However, I tell him I am on my way out
And he is already walking up to the door
But I tell him I can't stay I'm heading next door
Because I've been invited to a swimsuit party
And he asked me to borrow some trunks
Therefore, he can go along with me
And I tell him go pick out a pair on the bed
However, make it snappy so I can be prompt
As he rushes up and right back down
We head over and she greets us at the door
And my cousins mouth drops staring at her beauty
As I understand now what it means
To look through the eyes of a man

She invites us in and introduces us
To her family and friends
She offers us some food and drinks
As we start to mingle with the crowd
And my cousin heads toward one of her friends
As they begin to talk for hours & hours
And I become lonely standing there alone
Cindy heads toward me working her way through the crowd
As I picture her beautiful smile
And those light blue eyes & luscious lips
Down to those round hips moving back and forth
As the Hawaiian skirt hugs her all in the right places
And I cannot get over the scenery that is approaching me
As I look through the eyes of a man

Once she gets to me, she grabs my hand
And ask me if everything is ok
As she pulls me with her to take a walk
Nevertheless, I feel strange leaving with her
Because I don't want to upset any of her guest
As she escorts me down the shore
She ask me how am I enjoying the party
And I say it is going good for my cousin
Nevertheless, I am having an ok time
As the wind picks up and she starts to shiver
I take my shirt off and put it on her to keep her warm
And she thanks me and places my arm around her
I start to think of pulling her closer
As I look through the eyes of a man

We begin to head out of site of the party
As she stops to stare upon the moonlight shining
And she turns and gives me a hug & kiss
As my heart starts to beat fast
And my legs begin to buckle
As I fall down into the sand
And she reaches her hand out for mine
As she begins to sit right next to me
And moves in close to stay warm
As I look through the eyes of a man

As the waves crashes upon the rocks
While we sit under the stars
I turn and face her and look at her beauty
Shining under the bright light of the moon
And reach out and pull her close
As see falls deep into my arms
And she looks at me with tears in her eyes
Because she has some pain in her heart
And I ask her if she is ok
But as the tears begin to fall down her face
And all I can think about is holding her close
As I look through the eyes of a man

I try to console her to let her know its ok
And that I will be here, as long she needs me
Because as her tears fall I feel her pain
As I place her head upon my shoulder
And I squeeze her tight into my arms
As the moon shines brightly upon her
And the summer breeze blows through her hair
As she begins to settle her nerves
And wipe away the tears from her face
Because she says, we need to get back to the party

As I get up to wipe off and help her up
And she stares into my eyes with passion
Now I realize how love feels
Looking through the eyes of a man

We slowly walk back to her place
And join the others as the party goes on
She leans in and kisses me on the cheek
And thanks me for being her pillow
As she cried all of her pain away
And hope that she can repay me someday
Nevertheless, I tell her no repayment needed
As she starts to smile with a twinkle in her eyes
Because she feels safe and warm around me
As she walks toward the crowd
And turns back to look at me
She winks her eye and blows me a kiss
I cannot explain what I am feeling inside
As I look through the eyes of a man

I look at the time and its 4am
As I track down my cousin
And we say our goodbyes to everyone
As we head toward the door
Cindy grabs my hand and tells me to call her
And gives me a long hug and kiss
As my cousin is shocked with the event
And I exit the party with an unusual glow
As my cousin begins to ask 21 questions
However, I am in another world as we walk home
As he tries to snap me out of my happy place
All I can think of is Cindy
As I look through the eyes of a man

Faithful

I glanced across the room
As your smile caught my eye
Along with those luscious lips
And those sexy dimples
Just made my soul shake
As I approach you
And your friends
We engage in eye contact
As you whisper to your girls
Just as I move in close
Therefore, I can ask you your name
You tell me to do not play
With trying to be smooth
Unless I'm being Faithful

I lean in to tell you my name
As I tell you this is not a game
Because you seem precious
And worth the time
Then you say ok
As you, tell me your name
I then pursue to ask you
If you would like to dance
As you say yes
I take your hand
And escort you to the dance floor
As I ask you if you're spoken for
You tell me you have been
Single for eight months

And was giving up
On finding that special someone
That would treat you right
And be Faithful

We head back to the table
As we hold a deep conversation
Then you start to yarn
As you say, it is getting late
You start to say goodnight
However, I ask if we could
Exchange numbers
Therefore, I could call you sometime
However, you were hesitant
Because you had your doubts
That I was not being Faithful

I told you to give me a chance
As I promise you
That I will amaze you
She gave me her number
And said to me
Please do not play
With her emotions
And I said just wait and see
What I bring to the table
I promise I will not disappoint
Because I truly believe
You deserve someone Faithful

We have been talking for weeks
And you are coming around
However, you still have doubts
Therefore, I send you roses

On your job
And your girls are shocked
They cannot believe it
As you, receive your singing telegram
Of your favorite song
And I am just getting started
To prove that I'm Faithful

Your best friend said WOW
And ask if you
Are you going to take a chance?
On me to see if, I am for real
Nevertheless, you are still skeptical
Therefore, I make arrangements
With your girlfriends
To get you out to the club
As I get dressed
To meet you at the club
However, I stop to pick up
My surprise for you
I hope it proves to you
That I am serious
And prove that I can be Faithful

I walk into the club
And I spot your girl
She sees me and the plan begins
As you have your back to me
And I approach the table
I get funny looks

As I walk through the crowd
With your favorite stuffed animal in my arms
Along with your favorite chocolates
As your girl runs interference
And the DJ begins to play your song
I walk up behind you
As you turn around
You start to shed a tear
And at that moment
You realize that I am worthy
Because you feel, I can be Faithful

As you, give me a hug
And your friends cheer
I tell you are special
And I want to be
Everything that you dreamed of
And I will give you my all
Because I feel, you deserve it
And I want to be the one
That provides you happiness
And that security blanket
You dreamed of since
Being a little girl
And I promise to make
All of those dreams come true
And help you realize
That your great knight
Has rode in to the rescue
And will be Faithful

Feelings

I want to explain to you
How I feel about you
Sitting here thinking about you
Is clouding my mind
But now I know why I feel the way I do
Because you are everything
That I have been looking for my entire life
And it warms my heart
Because you listen to me
Care about how I feel
And can make me feel at ease
When things get out of hand
You know the perfect things to say
To help soothe my mind
And your soft spoken voice
Brings a smile to my face
And those are my feelings!

I wish things were different for you
Because I have so much to tell you
But having that private time
Just to talk to you is difficult
For just one night
I would sacrifice my time
Just to spend with you

And open up my heart to you
Just to let you know that my feelings are true
And how special you are to me
When I am spending time with you
And those are my feelings!

I know it may seem like infatuation
But I can tell you right now it is more
And whatever I feel I cannot hide
Because of your kindness, and big heart
Draws me closer and closer to you
And those are my feelings!

Find Love

The soul of a man is sacred
However, when he falls in love
It becomes a treasure chest
Full of great feelings for a woman
But if he can't find someone to share it with
Then he will become lonely
And never find love

Real men give women there all
However, phony men just play games
And hurt women's feelings
However, I am a real man
With a lot of love inside
But can't find a suitable partner
Because women have been played so much
That when a true man comes along
He does not get a fair chance to prove
That he is for real
And never find love

Love can hurt the soul
And bring you to your knees
But unless you are strong
You cannot survive the pain
Nevertheless, remember to stay strong
Because no matter how long it takes
Or if it ever happens
That special someone is near
And may have a lot of fears
However, once they control those fears
And they may not see the magic
That is within your soul
They may take a chance
On your feelings to be happy
Nevertheless, if not then they may fall short
And never find love

Fire Place

Looking down from the mountain top
But our skiing time
Is almost over
And I cannot wait
To return to the cabin
And get you dried off
As I gather wood
And start to set the fire
Therefore, we can drink coco
And snuggle real close
By the Fire Place

As we get comfortable
And watch the fire burn
We start to reminisce
About our first romantic
And steamy night together
It made me shiver
Because it was beautiful
And it made my knees buckle
By the Fire Place

Let me take you back
To that passionate night
With the rain falling outside
As were sitting by the fire
Holding each other close
As you whisper in my ear
Take me I am yours
And my eyes light up
As I prepare you
For your special treat
By the Fire Place

I lay the blanket down
Along with the pillow
Then I walk to the kitchen
And bring back the honey
For my sweet
As I stand you, up
And strip you bare
I then blindfold you
And lay you down
On the pillow & blanket
As the fire burns
And I open up the honey
By the Fire Place

As I pour the honey, up & down your body
And start to write with my tongue
My feeling for you
All over your body
You begin to breathe heavy
As you start to moan
I work my way up to your neck
And slide down to your breast
Continue down to your thighs
As your legs, lock me in
By the Fire Place

As the heat of the moment
Makes you scratch and moan
I lift your legs up onto my shoulders
And lick you behind your knees
Watching your toes curl
And having you gloss your lips
With the soft stroke of your tongue
I slowly place my hands
Upon your hips
And climb on top of you
As I place honey in my mouth
And start to give you a kiss
Your body starts to shiver
By the Fire Place

Ghost Left in My Heart

Lost love is the toughest thing to get over
But as I walk along the cruise ship
To clear my mind of this heartache
I cannot stop imagining you by my side
As I stare, off into the moonlight
I pray that I will survive this pain
That you have caused deep inside
As I try to shake away the pain
Of the ghost left in my heart

As the wind blows heavily upon my face
I hear woman voices approaching my position
However, I do not want them to see me cry
Therefore, I try to wipe away the tears
As the one notices my sadness
She stops by to see if I am ok
As she tells her friends to go on without her
And she can see the pain on my face
Of the ghost left in my heart

We begin to talk and walk along the deck
As she begins to rub her arms
Because the strong wind is making her cold
I take my jacket and put it around her
As she tells me that is so sweet
We head inside to the dining area
And her smile reminds me of my love

That I have lost with this burning pain inside
And it makes my eyes start to tear
Because I can't get off my chest
The ghost left in my heart

She tells me I look as though I lost my best friend
However, little does she know I did?
And it hurts more and more each day
Just knowing that she is gone forever
I do not think I can ever get that love back
However, she tells me a story about her
And what she has been through in her life
Because she knows the pain that, I am feeling
And that it will take a while to recover
However, she says as long as I do not let
It consume my entire soul
That one day soon, I will be able to shake
The ghost left in my heart

Give My All

As I sit and think about you and me
I can't help but wonder if it's true
But all I know my heart is torn
And I do not know what else to do
Because I feel lost each and every day
As you tell me, you love me deeply
I just cannot stop feeling insecure
Because your heart can change instantly
However, all I can do is stay prepared
Because every day I try to please you
As I give my all

Sitting here listening to my music
And thinking about the pain in my heart
However, all I can feel is the emptiness inside
Because at any giving moment you could leave
And the pain in my heart would deepen
As I hold onto the great times, we shared
But no matter what I can't shake the pain
As I begin to shut myself, off from the world
Because my soul wants to be all alone
And I cannot block out the pain inside
I think of all of the what if's
As I always, give my all

Golden Girl

I walked you to your car
And I had a craving for you
However, we still are feeling each other out
To see where our passion is leading
Because your lips are soft and pure
And your smile gives my soul the cure
For the pain that I have endured
Because you're my golden girl

I go to sleep with you on my mind
As I fall into a deep sleep
And begin to have sweet dreams about you
Your soft touch cast a spell on my heart
And it causes me to lust for you
But as the dream intensifies
As I begin to sweat and lick my lips
Because you're my golden girl

As your laying there next to me
And notice I cannot lay still
As you hear me whisper your name
You wonder what the dream is about
And want to wake me up
But you sit back and take notes
To see if the dream is about you
And not someone else
But as the dream continues
I reach out to you and pull you close
As I call your name out loud
And then you know I am only thinking of you
Because you're my golden girl

As I start to kiss you on your neck
You try to pull away
But the soft kisses makes you moan
And gets you all excited and wet
As you, proceed to wake me
I come around and start to rub your body
All over with slow motion strokes
As you, tell me not to stop
And I remove your shirt
As I kiss you upon your breast
Because you're my golden girl

As the early morning approaches
And we get each other worked up
We begin to let our bodies intertwine
As you, want me to have sex with you
But I refuse because you deserve better than that
And I will only make love to you
Because that is how special you are to me
And I want to please you the right way
Because you're my golden girl

As I make passionate love to you
You begin to gently bite along my skin
And that just kicks me into overdrive
Because it drives me wild
And makes me lose control of myself
But the pleasure that you're receiving
Cannot add up to what you are feeling inside
Because you're my golden girl

Good to the Last Drop

As I stare at you in your lingerie
I cannot control my emotional thoughts
As it makes my head spin round & round
And your beauty drives me wild
As your sweet sensual lips, call my name
And your pretty eyes put me in a trance
As my temperature begins to rise
And my heart skips several beats
Because of how you make me feel
As I fade into my dreams
And know that your good to the last drop

As you pose for the camera in style
And that luscious smile brightens the room
I cannot help but picture you in my arms
Because of how you make my knees shake
And how you make my nature rise
But all-in-all I'm at a loss of words
And I cannot stop staring at your curves
Because it wants to be caressed
And rubbed downed from head to toe
Because you are good to the last, drop

I cannot stand the anticipation of your kiss
As I reach, out and grab your hand
And I sweep you off your feet into my arms
As I begin to carry you to the bedroom
While you look at me and lick your lips
As you are anticipating the next step

Because I have, a master plan in my mind
As I lay you, down gently upon the bed
And slowly run my fingers through your hair
As you lay your head down upon the pillow
And gradually close your eyes in lust
As your body wants to be caressed
Because it looks good to the last, drop

I begin to stroke your body slowly with my tongue
As it makes your body quiver deep inside
That is just the beginning of a long night
As I kiss you from the top of your head
And down to the tip of your shoes
However, trust me there is more in store for you
As I remove your shoes and kiss each toe
And move up toward your private section
As I kiss you on both of your thighs
Because your body tastes good to the last, drop

As I lick you upon your stomach & belly button
And work my way up to both of your breast
As I begin to slip my tongue under your bra
And your nipples start to become hard
Because your hormones are kicking into overdrive
And it makes you dig your nails into my back
However, it just does not stop there for you
Because as I move toward your lips
And kiss you gently along your neck
As your body taste good to the last, drop

As our hot steamy night continues past midnight
And I move toward your sexy lips
Because the night is getting hot & heavy
As I slowly begin to caress your skin
And kiss you on your chin
As I proceed to kiss you on your cheek
And then upon your nose & forehead
However, that is just the beginning for you
As you, pull me close to your lips
And whisper in my ear don't stop
As I can only think of one thing
And that is how beautiful you are looking
As your body taste good to the last, drop

Grandmother

My Grandmother is one of a kind
You just imagine
How special she is to me
Throughout her lifetime
She has made a name for herself
By single handedly raising six kids
While she worked to put food on the table
And clothes on their backs
As she keep a roof over their heads
And managed to keep them on the right path
She should receive an award
For her effort and good will
Just for being my Grandmother

Although I'm the oldest grandchild
I wish her the best and much more
Because you are my #1 role model
Of all times because I love you
And the intelligence you possess
Along with the wisdom you demonstrate
I hope you pass onto me one day

Therefore, I can share with my children
And also my own grandchildren
As I explain to them how wonderful
That their great grandmother was to me
For being a part of my life
It always bring tears to my eyes
Because you're my Grandmother

It makes me the happiest grandson in the world
Just knowing God blessed me with you
And that I am your biggest fan
But saying this isn't enough for me
I hope that as times passes by
You bless me with your talent and skills
To be as lovely as you
I cannot imagine the day
When I can make you a great grandmother
Knowing deep inside my heart
You will always watch over us
Because of your big heart
And caring soul for me
I can only wish that I did you proud
As being your grandchild
And I will love you until I die
Because you're my Grandmother

When I look back upon the past
I will always see your pretty smile
No matter how bad things get in my life
I will gather the strength of your love
To help get me through the rough waters
That I may encounter in my future
However, I cannot think of anyone
That can ever take your place in my heart
Because you're my #1 role model in the world
And I cannot tell you how much
I respect you as a person
And honored to be your grandson
Because I love you, more than words can explain
And I wish you many more happy moments in life
Because you are my all, time favorite Grandmother

Love Always Your Grandson!

Green Eyes

As the alarm clock goes off at 5am
I begin to sit up on the side of the bed
And think back to our talk last night
Because I cannot get you off my mind
And it brings a smile to my face
Because I think, I am falling for you
However, I do not want to get ahead of myself
And jinx what we have right now as friends
But looking at your picture and those eyes
It gives me goose bumps down my spine
As I gaze deep into your Green Eyes

I cannot understand why you are single
Because you have all of the qualities, men want
And being a man I fantasize about you
Because you're beautiful inside & out
And you're seductive smile blows my mind
Because from head to toe you drive me wild
As I daydream of holding you in my arms
I fantasize more and more about you
As I'm hypnotized by your Green Eyes

I would love to take you out to dinner
Because I have a special, night planned
As I shower you with red rose petals
And we sip on some white wine
As I blow you, sweet kisses from my heart
And stare deep into your eyes
Because this is just the beginning stage
However, there is more in store for you
As I'm hypnotized by your Green Eyes

As I drive you, home for the night
You reach over and give me a kiss
And place your hand on my thigh
As we pull up to your door
And you invite me inside for tea
As you wink at me & lick your lips
I get nervous and begin to stutter
As you, pull me by my hand
And guide me through the door
I begin to tremble all over inside
And you begin to smile and stare at me
As I'm hypnotized by your Green Eyes

Happy Valentine's Day

Memories are outdated
However, just to see you again
Makes my mind spin
As I sit around & kick myself
Because you deserve better
And I hope and pray
That you are happy in the future
I wish I knew your feelings
Or what is going on in your head
However, I do not want to interfere
Because you have your life
And you seem so happy
All I want to say is
Happy Valentine's Day

This is a special day for lovers
And is celebrated by many
With love and compassion
Deep within my heart
I care for you
More than you will ever know
But things happen for a reason
Just do not forget the good times
Because there special to me
And with lots of hugs & kisses
All I want to say is
Happy Valentine's Day

Harvest Moon

Sitting here on the porch
As the sounds echo
Through the night
And a fall breeze is casting a chill
Upon my face
With you on my mind
And wishing you were here
To take in the bright light with me
Of the beautiful Harvest Moon

I imagine hearing your voice
As I pace back and forth
Along the porch of the cabin
I go and light the fireplace
And listen to the owls hoot
As I settle down in the chair
I picture you right next to me
Holding you close
As we rock in the chair
With your head on my shoulder
As we stare into the light
Of the Harvest Moon

Because of your job commitments
You said you could not be here
And our special weekend plans
Are not going to come true
And you were disappointed
Because I was here alone
And you were missing out
On the planned weekend
Under the Harvest Moon

Half of the night is gone
And I close my eyes
To get some sleep
Thinking our plans are ruined
And our weekend get away
Is going to end being apart
As I dose off into a good sleep
I dream I feel your gentle touch
And smell the wonderful scent
Of your perfume
Under the Harvest Moon

In my dream, I hear the sound
Of your lovely voice
And it seems to get closer
As I open my eyes and see my baby
Standing in front of me
Begging for forgiveness
With tears upon her face
And sadness in her voice
As I stand up
She reaches out to me
And gives me a hug
As she breaks down
And keeps saying she's sorry
However, I tell her it is ok
Because we are together now
As I hold her tight
Under the Harvest Moon

I start to comfort you
By telling you the night
Is still young & has just begun
As I lay you, down
In front of the fire place
And kiss you on your neck
As I gaze into your eyes
While the crackling sound
Of the fire goes dim
And the moonlight shines upon your face
You shake your head
And I ask what is wrong
But you stutter my name
And hope the moment never ends
Under the Harvest Moon

The passion turns up
As I run my fingers through your hair
And roll you over onto your stomach
As I break out the lotion
And massage you up & down
With slow gentle strokes
As I put you in a trance
And roll you back over onto your back
As you whisper softly to me to come closer
Under the Harvest Moon

I move in closer and you ask me
To make love to you
Because the mood is perfect
And you said making love
Under the moonlight
Is a fantasy of yours?
And I start kissing you
As the moon shines bright
And we begin to make love
As I think things, happen for a reason
Under the Harvest Moon

Heaven Sent

I think about you
All the time
And I cannot get you
Off my mind
And it drives me wild
However, I know it is just a dream
Because in reality
We do not have a chance
To be together
Because in your mind
You do not feel the same way
About me in your heart
I continue to pray
That your feelings change
Therefore, we can be together
Because your Heaven Sent

I crave for you
Day and night
Just to have you near
And to hear your voice
As I close my eyes
I picture your sexy face
And that lovely smile
That provides my heart
With joy and happiness
Because your Heaven Sent

As I stare at the ceiling
And think about
All the good times
We shared together
And how happy we seem
When were together
Because we feel safe
Around each other
Whether were smiling
Or shedding tears
Because it brings a sense
Of security and passion
That shows our strong connection
With one another
Because your Heaven Sent

Call me crazy
Nevertheless, I think about us
Being together as a couple
And getting married
Starting a family
And living happily ever after
Because God placed you
In my life for a reason
And I would like to explore
The reason why
Because we are so compatible

And we bring joy
Into each other's lives
And it seems like fate
But you keep shying away
Because this is new to you
And unchartered waters
For your feelings
And heart & soul
Because your Heaven Sent

Prizes are won
And feelings are earned
But what I feel for you
Brings me such devotion
That is why you
Stay on my mind
And you are etched
Into my heart & soul
And it feels good
When I can be humbled
By the very thought of you
And I only wish
That you felt the same
Because the love
I have for you
Is as real as your heart
Because your Heaven Sent

Heavens Above

As I stare across the table at my love
I reach out and take her hand
And escort her to the dance floor
Because the night is almost over
And I want this last dance with her
Because I want to hold her close
And tell her how much I love her
As I grip her tight in my arms
And look out upon the stars
As we prayed to the heavens above

I cannot picture me not with her
However, this is all a dream in my head
Because on one snowy night
I lost my life to a drunk driver
And it brought sadness to my love
As she was waiting for me to come home
However, she just received a knock at the door
And it was the police with the bad news
As they explained the situation to her
She just lost control of her emotions
As she cried for hours at a time
And she prayed to the heavens above

With family & friends close by her side
She just cannot believe that I am gone
And it gets harder and harder each day
Because she just waits by the door for me
To see me walk in and give her hugs & kisses

Nevertheless, she realizes I am definitely gone
She curls up with a pillow holding it tight
As her eyes fill up with tears
And they begin to stream down her face
She stands up & drops to her knees
As she prays to the heavens above

Now the day has come to put me to rest
And the family has gathered at the church
As friends and family, begin to pay their respects
And my best friend will read my eulogy
As she wipes her eyes that are full of tears
She thinks back to all of our good times
And cracks a smile along with her tears
Because she is still in shock of my death
She stands up to say some words
But as she pays her last respects
Her voice starts to fade in and out
As she says her final goodbyes
And prays to the heavens above

Honest

If only you knew, how much you mean to me
You make my head spin
And my heart skips a beat
When I am near you or thinking of you
I want you to know I am being Honest!

I thought the world of you
When you were around during the day
But now that you are next to me
My feelings are growing stronger
And I can't explain why you
Make me feel this way
But I do know one thing
My feelings will never change
Because I am being Honest!

Maybe one day you can tell me
How you really feel
But until then I can wait until you are ready
I will miss you with all my heart
Just being Honest!

If anything comes out of this, it happens
But that is my secret & promise to you
That it stays with me & only me
Just being Honest!

Just to give you my description of you
Says you are lovely from head to toe
And it drives me wild it might be wrong
But I do not want it to be right
Just being Honest!

Hot Tonight

The snow is falling outside the cabin
And the temperature is dropping
However, the fire is burning slowly
Therefore, it is keeping the room warm
Just as I am sitting there, you walk in
And our eyes connect as one
Nevertheless, those pretty blue eyes
Staring at me
Has my juices flowing inside
Because it is Hot Tonight!

You slowly walk toward me
And you start to smile
It causes my heart to skip a beat
As we lick our lips simultaneously
And our bodies start to shake
Because our emotions pull us closer
And closer into each other's arms
But our actions do not stop
Until we are face to face
Because it is Hot Tonight!

I move slowly to lock the door
Therefore, we do not have any interruptions
As we allow our passion to take over
And I stand you in front of the fire
As I whisper in your ear
And tell you what is in store for you
As I head to the kitchen to get the ICE
Because it's going to be a long night
And I hope you are ready to be satisfied

Because I packed my lunch for this moment
And I am taking you to the clouds
As I remove your shoes
And then your sweater
However, it does not stop there
As I remove your bra
And your pants & thong hit the floor
I walk you over to the love seat
Now it is time for your treat
Because it is Hot Tonight!

I sit you down gently in the chair
And place the ice in my mouth
As I passionately massage your feet
And place your toes softly into my mouth
As the ice falls in-between your toes
And the sweat starts to pour down your face
Along with the faint moan from deep within
You dig your nail into my back
And I know the feeling
Because it is Hot Tonight!

As I start to lick you from head to toe
You call out my name
And I pace myself from top to bottom
Making sure, I do not miss a spot
Because I want this night of passion
To be perfection in the making
And keep you yearning for more
From now until forever
So hold on tight your about to take off
And fly on cloud nine
Because it is Hot Tonight!

As your private area becomes wet
And your body starts to shine
With the sensation of our bodies touching
You say you are ready for sex
However, I still need to show you more
Because I want this to touch your heart
And never leave your soul
Because it is Hot Tonight!

As I place your legs over my shoulders
And lick you in a circular motion
As you, pull my head in closer & closer
Until you start to scream & moan
Because I hit your sensitive spot
And it makes you cum repeatedly
However, it does not stop there
Because I move up to your breast
And gently suck on your nipples
As the ice starts to dissolve
In-between your cleavage
And run down toward your belly button
As I catch the flowing water line
And work my way back up
Towards your breast
With the light stroke of my tongue
Because it is Hot Tonight!

As I roll you onto your front side
And start to lick you up & down
Your goose bumps arise
All over your back side
As I continue to kiss you
Up and down from your neck
All the way, down to the heel of your feet

And work my way back up
As I stop along your ass cheeks
And gently bite you from left to right
As you, begin to lose control
And grip the chair tightly
As you lay your head upon the pillow
And cannot wait for the love making to begin
Because it is Hot Tonight!

As you, push me onto the floor
And straddle over top of me
You ask me if I am ready
Because you want me now & later
And you place me inside of you
As you, slowly grind from side to side
Then up & down
Until you feel me deep inside
As you, press your hands against my chest
And call out my name
While you bite your lip
To control your emotions
Because it is Hot Tonight!

As you, place your breast in my face
I grab more ice for your nipples
And that intensifies the passion
Because you continue to go wild
And I tell you to put it on me
Because I want you to give it your all
As I call out your name
Because it feels so good to me
And that the night has just begun
Because it is Hot Tonight!

I pull you up to the chair
And you sit on top of my lap
As you, face the fire
I start to grind you in a circular motion
And you throw your head back into my chest
As I kiss you along your neck
And work my way over to your sexy lips
As I grip your ass tightly
And make you cum, as I am deep inside of you
Because it is Hot Tonight!

As I hold you up against the wall
And make mad passionate love to you
Our bodies start to join as one
And you dig your nails deep into my back
As that turns me on with every pinch
I continue to intensify my strokes
As the sweat starts to pour, off of my face
And you place your tongue in my mouth
Because it is Hot Tonight!

As we, both start to release ourselves
And make that last push for perfection
As we, both extend a loud moan
Because our bodies have hit the final stage
And our passion has intertwined
As we lay down in front of the fire
And snuggle real close
Because it is Hot Tonight!

I Love You

When I first met you
I knew you were special
Because your smile brightened the room
And your voice astounded me
Getting to know you was first & foremost
However, to meet you would be a blessing
That is why I Love You!

Wishing that we could be together
Is a complicated wish
Because we both belong to someone else
Even though that is true, we cannot hide
How we feel about each other
I know deep down inside my heart
Because destiny is knocking at our door
And our connection is out of this world
I know telling you this could cause problems
But I know that I Love You!

We need sometime alone to work this out
I know that being alone can make things worse
Nevertheless, I am willing to take that chance
Just to open up my heart
And I hope that you are too
Then I can prove to you
That I Love You!

The day that I kissed you
I knew I went too far
And I would like to apologize
For my selfless actions
I just hope that you can forgive me
And do not think I am a bad person
I would never want to hurt you
Because I Love You!

I feel this way because you blow my mind
And my heart beats fast when you are around
Your gentle touch sends chills up my spine
And your silky smooth skin drives me wild
While the twinkle from your eyes
Makes me yearn for you
And your luscious lips calls my name
Making me want you more & more
That is why I Love You!

I Miss U!

As I sit by the fire
I dream about being next to you
Every night I watch the stars
Twinkling in the moonlight air
And wishing you were here
To comfort my lonely heart
Reminiscing about the times, we shared
And spent in each other's arms
Your tender smile warms my heart
When were not together
I pretend to be happy
As I sit here all alone
I realize how much
I Miss U!

Two weeks have passed
And I am still missing you
As I watch the rain fall down
I remember the times
We often played in the rain
For hours before heading inside
To change then snuggle by the fire
Therefore, we would not catch cold
Sipping on some wine
As I gaze into your eyes
Just hoping the night would never end
As I start to shed some tears
I snap out of my dream
And I realize how much
I Miss U!

As I begin to write you another letter
I get a knock at the door
And as I open the door
It is you standing there
And I cannot wait
To hold you in my arms
As I squeeze you tight
I tell you face to face
How much I Missed U!

I Want To Be Naughty, Do You?

It is getting late
And the time has come
For me to explore your mind
And try to make contact
With your naughty side
Because we both like to take risk
And it is so exciting for us
However, just making you blush
Makes your beauty more than skin deep
It makes me want to be naughty, do you?

Taking my occasional midnight stroll
Helps me focus on myself esteem
Because everything I tell you
It is all true
Nevertheless, for you it is hard to believe
Because you haven't experienced
This type of adventure in awhile
But do not worry its ok
Because there's no pressure to respond
I just hope you can stop avoiding me
And let me discover your true feelings
Because if I judge you by your actions
You are strongly tempted
By your intrigue & adventure
Because I want to be naughty, do you?

What I see in you
Is a well rounded young lady
Just by the soft sound of your voice
And your golden smile

Attached to that beautiful face
Which drives me wild?
Because of your seductive charm
I want to be naughty, do you?

When I am with you
My temperature tends to rise
But I treasure our friendship
And I try to control myself
Because it's the gentleman in me
Not to over step my boundaries
And cause animosity between us
Therefore, I stick to just having you blush
Even though I can be bad
But if you feel differently
Then I am expressing to you
I would like to know
Because I want to be naughty, do you?

You told me I know how
To make you blush it's beautiful
It is not what I put on paper that's beautiful
Because when I'm describing you
I am being sincere
And I do not know what else
I can do to prove it to you
But by the end of time
I will try to accommodate you
With my sensitivity & admiration
However, I will always respect you
Because I want to be naughty, do you?

Sit back and let your mind dream
About me serving you a candle light dinner

With your favorite cocktails chilled on ice
As I take your hand
And escort you to the table
As I place you gently in the chair
And place the napkin across your lap
However, I almost forgot the main ingredient
And that is to kiss your hand
As I play 1 of your favorite songs
I promise to make it a night to remember
As I ask you to dance
And start the mood off right
Because I want to be naughty, do you?

Taking you on a moonlight stroll
Because having the stars above
Brings out your silky smooth skin
And the ravishing twinkle in your eyes
But let us not forget about your lips
Because there like two strawberries
So nice and sweet
But I could go on for hours
Because I want to be naughty, do you?

I think right about now
Your face is very red
But if you thought this is bad
You have not seen anything yet
Therefore, I will leave it up to you
To put the puzzle together
It should have you blushing more
But before I sign off
You should realize
That I want to be naughty, do you?

I Will Not Give Up On You

I cannot get you off my mind
Because how I feel for you
I want to pour out
My heart to you
Just so you know
I am for real
And I love you
But it is hard
When you do not feel
The same as I do
But just to let you know
I will not give up on you

Things have changed
And I do not know why
Because it's bothering me
Deep down inside
And I am sorry
For any pain
I may have caused you
But just know this
You hold a special place
Within my heart and soul
And I will not give up on you

If You Need Me

I know I came on strong
But that is how I feel
And I hope it never changes
Because deep down inside
I will always have a special place
In my heart for you
Because if I had to wait forever
I would have taken that chance
But if it never happens
I will always be here if you need me

Things for you are getting better at home
Therefore, I will back away from you
And this will be the last time
I will bother you with this non-sense
Because I feel like I invaded your space
And I do not want that to be the case
But over all you are still lovely to me
And if you ever need anything at any time
I will always be here if you need me

*Your other half is lucky
To have someone as special as you
Because a heart like yours is a dime a dozen
And that makes you special
Not just on the outside
But also on the inside
Because you are so understanding
And willing to give second chances
If things get out of hand
And that is very important in life
Because without people like you
There would be no me
But just remember if I make it big
You will be the first to know
Because you're special to me
And if you ever need anything just let me know
Because I will always be here if you need me*

I'm Sorry!

You seem to be distant lately
I hope you are not mad at me
Because if you are tell me why
Whatever it is please let me know
Because I can feel you slipping away
And that is not what I want
But it is not up to me to make that decision
Just so, you know I'm sorry1

I will do whatever it takes to make things right
But until I know the situation, my hands are tied
Can you open up and tell me what is wrong
But if I caused you any displeasure
I'm sorry!

You know you are the sun and the moon
That brightens my days & nights
But knowing you are unhappy breaks my heart
If I can change anything at all, let me know
Because I will do anything to make it right
Just letting you know I'm Sorry

J.A.M.I.E.

Spending time with you brings me joy
And holding you close
To snuggle with you
Makes my heart feel safe
However, I know there is still some doubt
About if, this is what you really want
But deep down in my heart
I want you no matter what
Because I can't stop thinking of you
J.A.M.I.E.

The time is going to come
When questions need to be answered
Because we can't go on
And put our lives on hold
If we're not going to give us a chance
Because it will not be fair
To either one of us
Knowing the circumstances
That it will lead too
Because I can't stop thinking of you
J.A.M.I.E.

It seems evident that were happy together
However, that does not mean a thing
If we know it's just physical lust
Because it can make or break us
And I do not think we are willing
To throw in the towel on each other
However, we need to realize that
This could be tricky to understand
Nevertheless, I know what I am feeling for you
Because I can't stop thinking of you
J.A.M.I.E.

JC Crazy

These past few weeks have been tough
Because of the pain, I have caused you
And every day that we are apart, I miss you
No matter what I see, you are hurting
And I want to make it right for us
Because I know now that, I messed up
And you have every right to hate me
However, I promise you this I will change
And be the man you knew from the start
Because I need you in my life
I will understand if you move on without me
And I pray for another chance for us
I will never let you down ever again
Because my heart is JC Crazy

I know that believing me is the last thing on your mind
Even though I know, the trust is gone
As the pain digs deep in your soul
I will do whatever it takes to make it right
Even if it takes me into another century
I will take that risk on you and me
Because you are worth every moment, that I have to wait
And my heart is lonely without you
Because every day that passes I think of you
And knowing I did you wrong without question
But as I sit and pray for your forgiveness
I know deep in my heart and soul
That I am JC Crazy

I know that you are truly broken inside
And I am sorry for all the heartache I have caused
I did not mean to hurt you at all
And I know this does not change a thing
Because you believed in me with your heart
And I let you down with a passion
As your heart is bleeding inside
And I hear the pain in your voice
I am also hurting inside with pain
Because I hurt the love of my life
And the most important thing to me
Because you were my special world
And I have not been the same since you have been gone
I miss you and love you more now than ever before
Because you are not in my life
And I am JC Crazy

I wish things were different with us
But I know that you are angry
And you need your space away from me
But so you know I do Love You!
And I always will no matter what happens
Because I messed up big time
And I cannot take it back or change the fact
But I will go through hell and high water
Just to make things right again with us
Because you're my sexy love
And I know it sounds bogus but it is true
Because I am JC Crazy

Keep Sake

As the sun shines upon the window pane
I begin to stretch as I get out of bed
As I turn to see you sleeping peacefully
I get up and head downstairs to the kitchen
And begin to make you breakfast
As I crack the eggs and start the toast
And begin to mix the pancake batter
As I chop up the fresh fruit
And pour you a glass of O.J.
I hope you do not wake up to the surprise
And that I can see the look upon your face
As I serve, you breakfast in bed
Because you're my keep sake

I open the door to our room
As you, begin to roll over
And your face tells the story
Because the smile on your face
Just lights up the room with joy
And you cannot believe the surprise
As I walk toward the bed with your tray
And you begin to sit up in bed
As I lay the tray upon your lap
You say thank you with a kiss
And all I can do is say you're welcome
Because you're my keep sake

As I hop in the shower while you eat breakfast
All I can picture is the joy on your face
And how wonderful it makes me feel inside
Because I know, you deserve much more
And I have a lifetime to prove it to you
However, breakfast is only the beginning
Because today is filled with many surprises
And I cannot wait to see your expressions
As I try and place you on a pedestal
And make you feel like my queen
Because you're my keep sake

Ladylove

As I approach the window to look outside
I see that the snow is coming down hard
And it is a beautiful site to see
But as I walk away from the window
I get a stiff chill that runs up my spine
And I head to the fireplace
To add more wood to the fire
As I rub my hands together
And sit down to continue my writing
As I see, lights pull up to the house
I jump up to see who it could be
And it is my ladylove

I hurry to the door to let you in
As I reach the door, you are standing there
And I pull you in to get you warm
As I help, you remove your coat
And your body is shivering cold
As I lead you to the fireplace
And wrap my arms around you
Because my body heat can thaw you, out
And there is nothing I like better
Then too please my ladylove

Let Go

Baby, where do we go from here?
Do we just let go
And forget about the love
We still share in our hearts
On the other hand, do we just let go
And let our lack of communication
Take us under with sorrow
On the other hand, do we just let go
And let the doors shut on our lives
While the pain grows deeper
On the other hand, do we just let go
And walk away without turning back
Realizing it is just finished
On the other hand, do we just let go!

We both know what it is like to be apart
However, I am going to honor your decision
And just let go
However, I hope you know I love you
With all my heart
As I grant you your wish
And just let go
Because of the living arrangement
I will try to avoid you at all cost
And just let go
Nevertheless, please do not let me stop caring
Or loving you
As I let go!

I know now that it is over
And I just want to apologize
For the unhappiness I may have caused
As I let go
We have been through a lot
And all things that were good
Always come to an end
I love you always & forever
Just do not forget that ever
Because this is my last, time bothering you
As I let go!

Lollipop

Someone as sweet and kind as you
Deserves to know what this means
Just use your imagination
And it will give you chills
Just hoping that the time we share
Will provide you with thrills
There are some steps involved
So sit back and enjoy the ride
And I will provide them for you
My sweet Lollipop!

First things, first we start with a kiss
And slowly get undressed
As I walk over and carry you to the bed
Just wearing a towel
And start to place you softly in position
For your massage as I whisper in your ear
And have you close your eyes to relax your mind
Then gently run my fingers through your hair
And massage your neck with smooth passionate strokes
As I turn back the towel until it stops at your hips
I lotion my hands and start to massage your back
This is just the beginning
My sweet Lollipop!

It seems to me that you are shivering all over
So check out what is next
I slowly roll up the towel to the bottom of your butt
And then prepare the lotion
To start to massage your thighs
Working my way down to your calves
Then down to your feet
Slowly repositioning your towel
As I turn, you over making sure your eyes stay closed
Before I continue to massage your breast
My sweet Lollipop!

I turn down the lights
And slowly remove your towel
As I begin to lick, you up & down
Then prepare the ice for each section
Of my lollipops curvaceous body
I start with a cube along your toes
And work my way up to your thighs
Then work my way up to your private spot
However, keep in mind this could take all night
So lay back and enjoy what is in store
Because you are my sweet Lollipop!

Lonely Heart

As the lightning strikes and the rain comes down
And the wind blows through the trees
As my mind is thinking of you girl
Just hoping that you are ok
As I wish, you were here with me
Therefore, I can kiss you all over
As I hold you tight in my arms
And we sit on the porch and watch the storm
Because I have a lonely heart

Two weeks have passed since I have seen my baby
And work has kept me busy day & night
However, I miss your beautiful soft skin
And the sound of her sexy voice
As she calls out my name
And I miss her sensitive touch
Because it drives me wild
As I think about all of her kisses
To help me comfort my lonely heart

Lose Control

As I dim the lights as we enter the room
I reach out to walk you over to the fireplace
And the sweet scent of the roses fills the air
As we sit down to enjoy the flames
You move in close and kiss me on the neck
And the wonderful touch of your lips
Makes my body tingle deep inside
As my eyes roll back in my head
And I imagine in my mind what is next
You start to remove my shirt
And gently rub my chest up and down
As I lose control

I slowly rub your thighs up and down
As you lick your lips and arch your back
And I raise your hand toward my mouth
As I begin to kiss each finger softly
And you begin to whisper my name
As I remove your tank top
And reach back to undo your bra
As the room starts to heat up
And our bodies begin to sweat
As we lose control

I pull you up out of the chair
And unbutton your jeans
As they drop down to your ankles
And you step out of the jeans onto the rug
As I lay you, down in front of the fire
And begin to kiss you from head to toe
As you, place your legs on top of mine
Because the night of passion
Is in the air and ready to begin
As we lose control

Lost In Feelings

It's a warm breezy summers evening
And the clouds are moving gently above
As you can hear the sounds of the state fair
And the sweet smell of fresh popcorn in the air
As I walk out upon the front porch
I hear a knock at the door
And it is my friends standing there
Just waiting to go over to the state fair
And have some fun, laughing and playing games
As the time passes us by
Not knowing that this is the day
That I will become lost in feelings

As we wait in line to throw darts
I glance over my shoulder
And I cannot believe my eyes
It is the one time love of my life
Standing in a distance with her friends
And she looks sad and unhappy
So as I get out of line to walk toward her
I catch her attention and her eyes light up
As I move closer to her through the crowd
It seems that she becomes lost in feelings

She begins to walk toward me
And I have so many things to say to her
However, I do not want to give her the 3rd degree
As we reach out to give each other a hug
She squeezes me tight as though not to let go

And I tell her how much I have missed her
Because I dreamed of being with her
For years and years with her in my life
Because I feel lost in feelings

She begins to pull away with the look
Of guilt upon her disappointed face
And I ask her how things are going
However, she just decides to walk away from me
And I follow behind her asking her what is wrong
As she begins to scurry faster away
I drop down to one knee and shout aloud
To her will you marry me in front of everyone?
Because I feel lost in feelings

As the crowd gets quite and she stops
Then turns around to see me on one knee
Her eyes begin to fill up with tears of joy
And I tell her that this is true from my heart
Because I always believe that, we belonged together
And I am willing to do what I can
To make her the happiest woman on this planet
If she just answers my proposal
And she slowly walks toward me
As she puts out her hand and says yes
Because we both have been through ups & downs
Now we do not have to be lost in feelings

Love and Hate

As I sit listening to my music
You continue to run through my mind
Because I see your pretty smile
And hear your sexy voice
Just flashing over & over in my mind
How you toyed with my emotions
Just put a dagger in my heart
And makes me feel for you
Love and Hate

I wanted to give you the world
Nevertheless, you did not feel the same way
And it is a shame plus your loss
Because I wanted to make you happy
Instead, you chose to lead me on
And use me as your security blanket
Just not realizing the pain I feel
And the scar that has been put on my soul
It just makes me feel for you
Love and Hate

I cry just as all men should
However, I hope you find happiness
And not the pain and disappointment
Because your security blanket is torn
And can't be repaired with sorry
Because what you did to my heart & soul
Just cannot compare to what I had to offer
And was willing to give to you
Now you see how it feels
It just breaks your heart
Because I wanted to be the one
And you never gave it a chance or risk
Now I know where I stand
And what I feel for you
Which is Love and Hate?

Love Is Not For Me

Take me to a place where dreams come true
Because all I get in life is heartache
It seems to happen more than not
However, as time passes by it gets harder
Because I just do not want to hurt anymore
I just cannot take any more pain
All I ever have done is give a women my heart
And it keeps being shredded to bits
As I treat them, how I thought they wanted to be treated
Nevertheless, love is just not for me

I see other couples hold hands and laugh
And smile, kiss and hold each other close
Nevertheless, I get knocked down every time
And my heart is getting weak from all this pain
I receive repeatedly from women
As I just do not know, why it happens to me
However, it is time for me to get a fresh start
Soon as the economy changes, I am gone
Because I refuse to go through more pain
I know deep down inside love is not for me

Love You and Hold On

Baby, why do you hide your feelings for me
Because it breaks my heart that you
Hide your feelings for me
And I cannot understand the game
That you play in your mind and heart
Because like they saying goes
You never know what you have until it's gone
And girl I don't want anyone else
However, the way things are going
I will have to let you go
And allow myself to be happy
With someone that is willing to love me
Nevertheless, do not ever think I did not try
To just love you and hold on

Everyone sees our feelings for one another
However, you continue to want to be independent
And you cannot commit to me at all
Then you also do not want me
To be with anyone else in life
Because of how you feel for me
However, you must realize in your heart
That you cannot have your cake and eat it too
Because all I want to do is, be with you
To just love you and hold on

*If fear is what is holding you back
Then you need to ask yourself
What can I do in my mind to conquer?
The fear of mine that keep causing me
To be confused in my heart & soul
Because I want to be wanted by him
And the times we share beings me joy
Because all he wants to do is, be with me
To just love you and hold on*

Luscious Beauty

As I stroll along the shore
To clear my mind
I run into a beautiful woman
That captures my soul
From head to toe
As she says hello
I start to stutter
And she just smiles at me
As her smile lights up
The midnight sky
Because she's a Luscious Beauty

As we pass by each other
We continue to look back
As I stop and turn
And walk toward you
You turn around and stop
As I get closer to you
You let your hair down
Into the lite summer breeze
As I get a few steps away
We exchange names
Along the shore
Because you're a Luscious Beauty

As we stare at one another
We know each other by face
But not by name
And we think back
To exactly how
And we remember
That it's through
Our other halves
Which were both trying to get over?
And I think that its fate
Because we felt
An instant attraction
Back then and even now
And all I can picture
Is your Luscious Beauty

As we talk to get acquainted
We take a romantic stroll
Along the Florida coast
As the breeze picks up
And I notice you are cold
I put my arm around you
And your face lights up
With that lovely smile
As you lay your head
Upon my shoulder
And you feel safe & warm
All I can see
Is your Luscious Beauty

As I escort you home
And walk you to the door
You give me a long hug
And a kiss on the cheek
As you, say Thank U
And you hand me a card
With your number on it
And tell me to call sometime
As I say, I will
And watch the door close
All I can think about
Is your Luscious Beauty

As morning comes
I get a knock at the door
As I answer the door
It is you standing there
As beautiful as ever
However, you have tears in your eyes
And you run into my arms
Because you feel safe
As I hold you, close
I say things will be ok
And you cry even more
Nevertheless, I will not let you go
Until I know, everything is ok
Because I can only picture
Your pretty smile from last night
And your Luscious Beauty

You gather yourself
As we begin to talk
And you tell me the problem
About your ex
And how he treated you
However, you are scared
And I said don't worry
Because you're in good hands
And no harm will come to you
As long as I'm here
Because I want to see
That sexy smile
Connected to your Luscious Beauty

You ask to stay with me
For a few days
And I say yes
As I help, you go grab something's
And I give you my room
As I set up the couch
For me to sleep on
And you refuse to take the room
Nevertheless, I want you
To be comfortable
And relax that lovely body
Of yours from top to bottom
Because I want to see
That lovely smile
Upon that Luscious Beauty

As we watch the sunset
Along the shore
You take my hand
And lead me to the couch
As kneel in front of me
And say that you are blessed
Because I'm your angel
Sent from up above
To protect you from harm
And that you are grateful
To be here with me
And that your soul
Is smiling deep inside
Along with your Luscious Beauty

As you, dim the lights
And snuggle close to me
As you stare into my eyes
And the tears begin to fall
You tell me this is a dream
Because your dreams don't come true
Nevertheless, I assure you they do
Because I'm here now
That is all that matters
Because I will make all of your dreams
Come true from this point forward
And put a smile
On your face
And make you feel safe
Because you deserve better
And you are my Luscious Beauty

I wipe away your tears
And you pull me close
Therefore, you can give me a kiss
And hold me tight
As your heart skips a beat
And your gentle touch
Makes me melt in your arms
As I enjoy these feelings
I imagine the wind
Blowing through your hair
The stars shining on your face
As I watch, you walk
Along the sand
Because you're my Luscious Beauty

You snap your fingers
And I come back to earth
Therefore, I can see your smile
And continue to ride
On cloud nine with you
Because you're so precious
And it feels just right
To be next to you
Under the stars
And holding you tight
As we watch the waves
Crash against the rocks
As I take a deep, breathe
Because you're my Luscious Beauty

Beauty is only skin deep
However, you have it all
Starting with your long curly hair
Down to your sensual eyes
Along with your lavishing lips
And slide down
To your curvaceous hips
And your luscious backside
Down to your incredible thighs
Last but not least
Your sexy feet
All the way, down
To those sultry toes
And I cannot explain
How you make me feel
But all I know
And all I think about
Is your Luscious Beauty

Luv

As you, whisper those words
My heart skips a beat
And my spine gets chills
As you, caress my soul
While the stars are bright
And the mood is right
It is time for Luv!

When were alone
You take my hand
And pray for another day
To be with me
And share our dreams
With the heavens above
As we hold onto our Luv!

It is now time to confess
To the whole wide world
And let it be known
That my heart is in it
And you are everything to me
Because you take my breath away
With your heart & soul
Because I know deep down
I am in Luv!

M.P.D. (Most Precious Desire)

Let me tell you a story
About what you do to me
When I stare at you
I lose control of my soul
And I dream about you
That is why you are my M.P.D.

I will take you by the hand
And tell you gradually
Why you drive me wild
From head to toe
Your smile brightens my heart
And to look into your eyes
Makes me melt like butter
With those luscious lips
Makes me stutter
Your hips put me in a trance
And your sexy feet
Makes my temperature rise
That is why you are my M.P.D.

I can image us being intimate
Because you deserve the works
Like a full body massage
To relax your mind
And make you feel at ease
That is only the beginning
As I kiss you gently all over
I have you close your eyes
As I place ice in my mouth

And start to lick you
Up & down all over slowly
And suck on your toes
As you, arch your back
And tell me don't stop
That is why you are my M.P.D.

The mood is set
And the journey continues
As I use my tongue
To write love notes
All over your body
With every gentle stroke
As you call out my name
And your heart skips a beat
While I yearn for you
As you pull me, close
And I fade into your arms
I cannot imagine our lives
Anywhere but here together
That is why you are my M.P.D.

Midnight Love

To be this far away
Is breaking my heart
Just hoping to be home soon
Means so much to me
Wiping the pain away
From my face
Makes me think of the days gone by
And the times we shared
During our Midnight Love

Midnight lovers share Love
To provide the romantic spark
In each other's lives
To keep alive the dreams
And feelings they hold deep inside

To be in your arms once again
Just makes me feel at home
And relieves the tension
That I have from being apart so long
Now that I'm on my way home
Back to comfort you
And see the chemistry
We have for each other
Makes me shed a tear
Just thinking about it
While staring out into space
I can just see what it means
To be in love
With someone so special

During our Midnight Love
Midnight lovers share Love
To provide the romantic spark
In each other's lives
To keep alive the dreams
And the feelings they hold deep inside

Now the wait is over
And I am making my move
To go see my baby
With some roses & perfume
Treat her to dinner
And a chilled bottle of wine
Whisper in her ear
And tell her I care
During our Midnight Love

Midnight lovers share Love
To provide the romantic spark
In each other's lives
To keep alive the dreams
And feelings they hold deep inside

As I gaze into your lovely
Dark brown sexy eyes
I see some confusion
And a lot of determination
To be alone with me
As we go down to the shore

And lay upon the sand
While the wind blows through your hair
And the waves crash against the rocks
While I hold you tight
And tell you I Love You
Over and over again
Then we start to make love
Making up for lost time
We have spent apart
As our bodies, intertwine
With the passion that is oh so sweet
As we continue until the crack of dawn
As we gather ourselves
During our Midnight Love

Mind, Body & Soul

Relax and free your mind
Because baby tonight
Will be a night you will not forget
Just lay your head down
And let the groove hit you
Because what you're about to witness
Will open up new horizons
For you and me baby
Just let me take you to the max
With the sensation you feel inside
Because I promise you girl
You will not regret the temptations
We both will receive from the Mind, Body & Soul

Baby, let me start with your toes
And massage your lovely feet
Work my way up to your thighs
And caress your hips with my warm touch
As I place my sweet lips
Upon your delicate skin
As I work my tongue in circles
Upon your belly button until you, say stop
Nevertheless, that is just what is in store
For your Mind, Body & Soul

Mine

All I do is daydream
About you girl
And it is blowing my mind
To see your smile
Just drives me wild
Knowing you're engaged
Makes my heart
Call out your name
And I know you cannot be mine
As the night goes on
I notice you are watching me
From across the hall
But I ask myself why?
Nevertheless, I can only imagine
That you must like me
However, it can also be my imagination
That is running wild
But something inside of me
Wants to make you mine

I just do not know
Why I am so attracted to you
Because you are spoken for
However, the way I feel about you
Seems like we've known
Each other forever
That is just a phase
That some of us go through
I would like to know
How you feel about me

However, I do not know
How to find out
Because a on the job rejection
Is the worst heartbreak
That anyone can suffer from
But I am not going to break-up
Something that will never be
That is trying to make you mine

Only one word describes you to me
That is Unique!
Because your smile lights up a room
And your baby blue eyes
Can charm a lion to sleep
With those two qualities
I just cannot put you out of my mind
If I had my choice
I will make you mine

Knowing it is just a fantasy
That haunts my soul
I know that life is full
Of fantasies and dreams
Some come true
However, relationships are not likely
To come out the way you expect
Them to turn out
I wish I could just come out
And ask you

What you think about me
Without having, you get upset
On the other hand, stop speaking to me
But I guess I will never know
What you think about me
I just know that whatever happens
I will always want you to be mine

Mother

I would like to dedicate
This to someone I love
And who is very close to my heart
She means so much to me
Nevertheless, I just cannot say enough
About this woman
That I would die for
But never the less
She is a strong role model
With the heart of a lion
And I would like to be just like her
And she is my Mother!

We are not as close as most children
And parents are but we survive
Maybe one-day things will be different
In the upcoming future
I owe her my life
Because if it wasn't for her
I would not be here today
Without her, I would be nothing
She made me what I am today
And I will always be grateful
To her for leading me down the right path
And for just being my Mother

Being a single parent is not easy
But if you can love a child
You can do just about anything
In this world to survive
And conquer all the headaches
As being a Mother

When I settle into my life
I would like to give back
Most of my success to you
Just to let you know
I owe you that much
With all the dedication and hard work
She put into me with her confidence
And the love to get me to the top
I cannot say enough about her
However, I just want to say Mom
That I Love You, I Love You & I Love You!
And you will be missed deeply when you are gone
So please stay with me forever
And be my Mother!

I Love You!
From Your Son

Mutual Love

Why do I continue to feel this pain?
And why do I continue to finish last
Because I'm too nice
And women prefer the bad boy type
But want to be treated right
And not cheated on and disrespected
Nevertheless, they choose the bad boy type
And end up getting hurt
Just like me I am overlooked
However, I will not change for no one
I just hope someday I can truly be happy
And find Mutual Love

I have giving my heart & soul in relationships
And I always seem to receive pain
But it happens to me being too nice
And if I was a bad boy
Then I would be considered a dog
But it seems women like men
To be rough around the edges
And people like me tend to suffer
Because were to nice
I just hope I find that someone
That will give me a fair chance
To find Mutual Love

I sit and wonder why sometimes
Then I shed tears
Because I wish to be happy
Just as much as the next, man
But I tend to attract the wrong women
And I keep receiving pain
Because I do all the gentlemen things
However, it seems to be not enough
And I never get a fair chance
However, I always get awe you are so sweet
That is fine & dandy
But it does not cure what I feel
Because it's not providing that special someone
To find Mutual Love

As the tears run down my face
And it helps release the pain
As I wish upon a star
And hope that I can be happy
Because constant heartache
Is not good for the soul
But maybe one day my pain & suffering
Will be wiped away
By that magnificent person
As we bring happiness to each other
Because then that someone appreciates
The true man inside of me
And we both find Mutual Love

My Blue Moon Turns To Gold

As I stare into the night
I call upon a star
To release all the pain
And to ease my broken heart
As the waves off the shore
Begin to stand still
I become lost in my thoughts
While I wish that my blue moon turns to gold

As I lay my head upon my pillow
I start to shed a tear
And pray to the one above
That I will give it my all
While I sit here all alone
And listen to my heart cry out
Wishing that my blue moon turns to gold

Hours have passed on this journey
And the pain is not gone
But my life is not over
As I sit here all alone
While my mind runs wild
And I lose my will to smile
Just hoping my blue moon turns to gold

My Heart Cries Out!

I met a lovely young woman
Standing about 5'2"
With a smile that glows at night
And the beauty of a queen
With dimples of a goddess
And dark brown hair
That makes my temperature rise
While my heart cries out!

The echo of your voice
Plays tricks on my mind
And I do not know what to do
I just cannot shake the sensation
That I have for you
You say nobody likes you
But you cannot even imagine
How attractive you are to me
If I can stop being shy
I would come out and explain
To you how I feel
While my heart cries out!

We have a lot in common
As we discussed in person
Maybe we can attempt to go out
If I can get up the courage
To ask you out sometime
But my shyness clouds my thoughts
As I start to clam up
While my heart cries out!

I have to snap out
Of this concept
And become more assertive
When it comes to you
Because I don't want
To let you slip away
And miss something good
If I don't react properly
I may lose this chance
To make myself happy
While my heart cries out!

But as I watch your every move
I can see you are a tease
Just trying to charm
Your way into my heart
With me taking the bait
I see it is a mistake
As my heart cries out

My Heart Desires

I sit here and fall into a daze
And think about my journey through life
Because I'm waiting for mister right
To come into my life and serenade me
And sweep me off my feet with love & affection
Because just the thought blows my mind
That the day is nearing when he arrives
To prove to my heart and soul
What my heart desires.

As I go out shopping for food
I walk up and down the isles
Picking up this and that
And head up to the checkout line
As I drop a can out of my cart
And what do you know it is you
The man in my dreams kneels down
To pick up my can of soup
Standing there in a cloud of shock
I say thank you with a smile
As you, touch my hand in the exchange
My soul knows what my heart desires

He begins to walk away but turns back
And walks back to me and pass me his number
He tells me that I am beautiful
And to call him when I get the chance
Because he likes what he sees
And I would like to know me better
As I blush as he walks away
I lose my train of thought
And can't regain my composure
But deep down inside my soul
I realize what my heart desires

My Soul Is Calling Out To You!

As the sunsets
Along with the summer breeze
I cannot get you off my mind
Because I miss you so much
Just waiting to hold you tight
And to kiss you all night
While I caress your body
And begin to swept you off your feet
Sit you down on the couch
And never wanting to let you go
Because my soul is calling out to you

I turn Marvin Gaye on
And I tell you how I feel about you
As I break down in tears
And you pull me close
Because you want me to feel safe
And I cannot control my tears
However, you tell me it is ok to cry
As I squeeze you tight
Because my soul is calling out to you

As I gather myself from the tears
I kiss you and do not want to stop
And I lift you up and place you on my lap
As I whisper in your ear
That you are everything to me
And I can't imagine being without you
Because my soul is calling out to you

Hours go by as were cherishing the moment
You take my hand
And lead me to the bedroom
As you, remove my shirt
You begin to crawl back onto the bed
And start to pull back the covers
While I remove my pants
As you lay your head on the pillow
And blow me kisses
You softly call out my name
As you, remove your clothes
And I lay down next to you
Because my soul is calling out to you

As I caress your body
While I make love to you
I wish that it never ends
Because I look deep into your soul
And tell you how much I care for you
As you, pull me closer
And whisper in my ear
That you are feeling the same excessively
As our bodies, connect as one
I cannot explain the joy I feel with you
Because my soul is calling out to you

Night Unfolds

As the rain falls
Upon the window pane
The moment is here
For me to light the fire
And start the mood off right
With Barry White playing
As we start to slow dance
Holding each other close
As I gaze deep into your eyes
Slowly I start to undress your body
And kiss you on your neck
I smell the sweet aroma of your perfume
That makes me lust for you
As the Night Unfolds!

As R. Kelly takes us on a 12-play journey
I start to run my fingers through your hair
With foreplay just around the corner
I start oiling your skin
With my passionate stroke
All over your body
While I gently kiss your toes
And start to take off
The oil with my tongue
As you start to moan
And call out my name
As I continue to lick, you up & down
You tell me you are ready
As the fire burns
Our bodies start to sweat
With our hearts beating as one
As the Night Unfolds

The clock strikes nine
And it is still early
As we sip on some wine
And caress under the sheets
I begin to tell you
What you mean to me
I wish time could stand still
While I'm with you
Because I care for you with all my heart
I would do anything to make you happy
Supply you with a rose a day
To keep your smile going for miles
And to let you know you are loved
By an extraordinary gentleman
As in myself
I want you to feel safe & warm
When you are next to me
No matter where we might be
In a restaurant, park, or at the movies
I just want you to think of me always
As the Night Unfolds

As we begin to shower
My mind starts to fade
And all I can think about
Is you in my arms?
As I reach, out and take your hand
I pull you next to me
And blow you a kiss
As you, catch it
And place it close to your heart
I start to shed a tear
As you, brush it away
With your gentle touch

As the water stops
I start to dry you off
As the Night Unfolds

As you, finish getting dressed
I have a surprise in store for you
As you, close your eyes
And I have you open them
You are in the state of shock
As you look at your gift
And you start to cry
As you try on your necklace
And you give me a big hug
You whisper in my ear
That you have a surprise for me
And its tickets for a cruise
As I give you a kiss
And pour us a glass of wine
I propose a toast
To the woman that is special
In my life and holds the key to my love
As the Night Unfolds

We go out on the town
To finish celebrating
And we go to our favorite club
As we approach the door
The surprises have just begun
We enter the club arm & arm
As we head to our table

Our song comes on
And we start to dance
All through the night
Until morning comes
The DJ makes a special announcement
And it is time for your final gift
To cap off our wonderful evening
As I get down on one knee
And propose to you live on stage
As you, accept my proposal
With open arms as you, tell me you love me
I ask you for this last dance
As the DJ ends the night playing
Boyz II Men (on Bended Knee)
While all good things have to end
As the Night Unfolds

On Our Side

As I heard your voice
I turned in shock
To see what caught my attention
As you approached the bar
I had one thing in mind
And that was to know your name
As you walked towards me
You began to smile
And I started to get nervous
However, I had to play it cool
Therefore, I asked you to dance
And you accepted my offer
As we settled on the dance floor
We exchange names
And began to converse
With time on our side

We decided to call it the night
As we exited the club
You passed me your number
And told me to call you sometime
As you get to your car
You blow me a kiss
And I almost died
With you on my mind I went home
As I opened the door
I pictured your face standing there
With your sexy brown skin
And luscious lips greeting me
With a hug and a kiss
Nevertheless, I shook off my fantasy
As I know, time is on our side!

The weekend is near
Therefore, I gave you a call
And you are not in the office
Therefore, I leave you a message
Nevertheless, you never return my call
And I feel rejected and hurt
Therefore, I decide to go out on the town
To clear my mind of you
And my homies are keeping me intact
While I try to overcome my pain
But as I sit here
I imagine your voice
As you, touch my shoulder
I realize it is you in the flesh
And you explain why you never called back
Therefore, you ask me to dance
And I was overjoyed
By your invitation & I lost control
And requested your favorite song
As the night went on
I knew then that time is on our side!

Once In A Lifetime

Love is calling our names
As we lay here next to each other
I look deep into your eyes
And I can see the tears inside your heart
Because you have strong feeling for me
However, there are obstacles in your way
That will not allow you to be with me
But you must realize you must be happy
For you and only you
Because true love can pass you by
Only happen once in a lifetime

I feel the joy you have when were together
And I see how you look at me
Because it is, love written all over your face
But you do not want to feel tied down
By having to feel obligated to say yes
For every time I may ask you to something
That is not the case
Because you will still be independent
And have your own personal time for you
But if that is, all you are worried about
You may want to rethink that decision
Because this true love ship can sail on you
And will only dock once in a lifetime

I see & hear the jealousy in your voice
As you, bring up other women
When it pertains to me
But you cannot have your cake & eat it too
Because we are just friends as you tell me
And I want more because of my feeling for you
But I must realize it is never going to be
Because unless you make that commitment
We will never be together as a couple
And I do not want to wait forever
Because I don't want to miss out
On the love of my life coming around
Because true love comes and goes
And may only happen once in a lifetime

Out of Control

Baby I try so hard
To be good to you
But all I get is an attitude
Time and time again
And I just do not understand
Why you wish to treat me this way
You say that you love me
Nevertheless, it is just a cover up
Therefore, you can have your cake and eat it too
However, I cannot handle the situation
Therefore, I am just releasing this pain
You are inflicting on me
Because you're out of control

My heart is fading away
From the love we once shared
I got the urge to call you
And it was a big mistake
Because some other man
Answered your phone
And that explained why
You had an attitude towards me
Therefore, I hung up the phone in shock
Sitting hear all alone
While your being entertained
By another lover
Now I know you are out of control

The truth has come out
I feel like a sucker
To let you suck me in
And walk all over me
My friends tried to warn me
But I just did not listen
Therefore, I went ahead
And got my feelings hurt
By a pretty face and a smile
Just to find out
You are out of control

Weeks have gone by
And I am still distant
From my friends and family
While I sit here feeling sorry for myself
And some of my friends
Try to get me out of the house
Nevertheless, I just will not budge
They understand my situation
However, I know it is not the end of the world
And I finally open up
As my friends stand by my side
While I go through this phase
In my life caused by you
And I still care for you
Nevertheless, I know you are out of control

To be hurt as many times
As I've encountered in my life
I have picked up a six sense
So when I am in a relationship
I can pick up when something's wrong
As if, my partner is being unfaithful
Because you can never under estimate
The powers of a woman
She can be as devious as a man can
When it comes to feelings
So from now on, I will be more careful
When I pick women
So let this be a lesson to all
When you fall in love
Make sure it is true love
And that it is not a joke
Because if you get hooked
You could wind up with
A woman who is out of control

Out of my Life

As the sunsets upon the window pain
I cannot get you off my mind
Because I know that, you are gone
And it was my entire fault
Because of me treating you bad
And you finally had enough
As you could not take the pain
And just walked out of my life

Sorry will not help ease your pain
I hope someday you will forgive me
Because I made a serious mistake
And it cost me my entire world
But as the time passes day by day
I never realize how much I loved you
Until you walked out of my life

They say that you will never know
How good you have it until it is gone
And I see the pain on your face
That was caused deep in your heart
By me not paying you much attention
And placing you second over everything else
Now I realize that stupidity
Brings pain to the ones you love
That is why you walked out of my life

Passionate Kiss

As I walk along the path
And head toward the house
As the summer rain
Beats upon my face
And the stars shine bright
Just can't wait to see you
And hold you close
As I give you a passionate kiss

As you open the door for me
You can't believe
That I'm soak and wet
As you pull me inside
And go grab me a towel
As you start to dry me off
And help me remove my wet clothes
So I don't catch cold
As you stare into my eyes
And I lean towards you
To give you a passionate kiss

As I wrap up into the towel
And light the fireplace
So we can keep warm
And get comfy and cozy
As we sit by the fire
And hold each other close
As the rain hits upon the roof
And I start to rub you down
As I give you a passionate kiss

As I run my fingers
Through your hair
And kiss you gently
Along your neck
As I send goose bumps
Up and down your spine
As I tickle you with my tongue
In all the right places
And dip your head
Into the pillow
As I give you a passionate kiss

The clock strikes twelve
And the passion evolves
Into hot steamy love
And we both wipe
The sweat from our brows
As we fog up the windows
And the impulse from our bodies
Breaks out into a sweat
As I lick you all over
Then the fire in your eyes
Calls out to me
As I give you a passionate kiss

Past Love

The walks we used to take
The fun we had out on dates
Brings a smile to my face
Whenever I think about her
I have to remember
She's my past love
That will never go away
She's my past love
That I still love today

The hours we spent on the phone
So neither one of us would be alone
Talking about this and that
It really didn't matter
To hear your voice
Would turn my gray skies blue
To not have you
I really don't know what I would do
But I realize now
She's my past love
That will never go away
She's my past love
That I still love today!

It's been six months
But I still have pain
I still take my walks
But now in the rain
Since we've been apart
I just can't get you off my mind
With the love I have for you
I seem to be obsessed
With my abnormal behavior
Toward the relationship we once shared
The disbelief of it being over
Is hurting me inside
I sit and wish that one day
Your feelings will change for me
And you will become my one
And only past love

Day by day I wonder
Why I feel this way
But I can't shake this sorrow & pain
That you left deep in my heart
But I have to move on
And realize that you're gone
But you will still be remembered
As my one and only past love

Prayer for Grandma

I am very lucky to have you in my life
Because you always was my hero
And if I haven't told you lately
I love you more & more each day
And there is not a day that goes by
That I do not think of you
And all what you have done for me
Because of you I am truly blessed
And this is my Prayer for Grandma

As a child you took care of me
And held me close when I was sick
You punished me when I was bad
And comforted me when I was sad
Nevertheless, the most important part you loved me
And for that, I felt safe and warm
Because you cared for me like no other
And through tough times, you gave your all
Because of you I am truly blessed
And this is my Prayer for Grandma

I sit alone and think about you
And I begin to cry tears of joy
Because you mean the world to me
And I do not know what I would do without you
I try and not think about you not being here
Because you are, the rock that keeps me grounded
But I just want you to be proud of me
And to know that I didn't disappoint you
But I know that I am not perfect
And sometimes you did not approve of my choices
But I know deep down inside you loved me
No matter what choices I may have made
Because you stood by me at all times
And I feel truly blessed that you are in my life
Because this is my Prayer for Grandma

Precious Moment

During every passing year, I see your smile
I think of how lucky I am to have you
Because you have watched over me
And I know you are so proud of me
However, more than that I am proud of you
Because you are treasured in my heart
And I have been blessed to be your daughter
Because God has provided me with my angel
And that person is my friend, my confidant and my Mom
Because you are my Precious Moment

Words cannot express enough of how I feel
Because with each passing day
I love you more and more
And that fills my soul from head to toe
Because you have provided me, love
And I always know I could count on you
Through all the good and bad times in my life
Because you always have my back
And I am grateful for your support
Because you are my Precious Moment

Standing in front of my family right now
Just makes me want to shed some tears
Nevertheless, I want to hold back until I am done
Because what I'm saying is true
And I know that we take things for granted
But with you in my life I could not ask for anything more
Because you bring me joy when I am sad
And you know exactly how to make me smile
As the walls, seem to be closing in on me
Because you are my Precious Moment

Pretty in Pink

I can't wait to get home to you baby
Because we've been apart for months
And I cannot get you off my mind
As the time draws near
That I will be able to kiss you
And hold you close & never let go
As my heart begins to cry for you
And I cannot wait to see you
Standing in front of me
In the gift that I sent you
Looking so pretty in pink

As I approach the door to enter
I begin to get cold feet
Just hoping you have missed me
As much as I have missed you
I unlock the door and to my surprise
You are already expecting me
As I stare deep into your eyes
And we run into each other's arms
I lift you up and squeeze you tight
As I place you down to kiss you
I notice how much I missed you
Standing there so pretty in pink

You begin to lead me to the couch
And sit me down to give me a kiss
As you, tell me to close my eyes
And you have a surprise for me
That will make my mouth water
And make my heart skip a beats
Because whats in store will blow my mind
As you, tell me its something pink
And just knowing that pink is my favorite color
Gets me very excited and anxious to see
Because I know, she looks pretty in pink

As she tells me to get ready to open my eyes
I pick up her perfume scent that drives me wild
As she reaches, out and touches my hand
And then tells me to open my eyes
As I slowly open my eyes, I am speechless
With the site that I am witnessing
Because the pink lingerie that she is wearing
Does not compare to what I sent her
And let me tell you pink is my color
And wow does she ever look great
Standing there pretty in pink

Rain

Its wet and I cannot sleep
Because the pain is too deep
And I hope it will end
However, my dreams are gone
Because you broke my heart
And I will never love again
Because of the pain deep inside
As I wipe away the Rain!

By the next morning
I cannot even think straight
Because I feel all this pain
That you placed upon me
And it is eating me alive
Nevertheless, I have to be strong
And fight the pain
As I walk away from the Rain!

Time is too short
To be hung out to dry
Because all my life
I've been walked upon
Now it is my time
To search & destroy
The pain in my heart
As I walk away from the Rain!

Raindrops Fall

As the wind begins to blow the curtain
And I walk toward the screen door
I pull the drapes back and look upon the sky
As the clouds, turn the sky gray
And flashes flicker through the air
Just as the rain begins to pour
I start to close the windows
And begin to set up candles to light
Just in case the power goes out
As I sit down by the cozy lit fire
Watching the raindrops fall

I am hoping that you are ok
And that you are keeping dry
As I picture you in my arms
Snuggling up in front of the fire
As I pour you a cup of tea
And make you feel safe & warm
As I begin to rub your back
And massage your shoulders
To make you relax as the thunder rumbles
Across the pitch black sky
As we watch, the raindrops fall

S.W.C. (Sexy White Chocolate)

All we do is flirt
And it feels so good
Nevertheless, we have other commitments
And it makes things complicated
Because we have an attraction
And if time presented itself
Depending on the case
We might take a risk
Nevertheless, I am happy for now
With you being my S.W.C.

I pick the wrong women
And that complicates things
Because I never find the women
That will care for me
Like I want them too
But when I find that person
There always spoken for
And it becomes difficult
Because of the attraction we feel
And the risk is too great to chance
Nevertheless, I am ok for now
With you being my S.W.C.

Scared

Driving along this country road
As the snow continues to fall
And the winter air begins to howl
As I am getting close to, home
And I cannot wait to see your smile
But as I pull up to the house
I notice your car is not there
And I begin to worry about you
Just knowing the weather is bad
And you are not home and there are no tire tracks
Showing signs that you were here
As I call your cell and there is no answer
I begin to worry more & more
And I go inside to see if there is a note
Because I'm scared

As I unlock the door and turn on the light
I see a note on the fireplace
As I walk to pick up the note to read
And I start to read the note
My knees begin to shake and become weak
And you are telling me that it is over
However, you could not tell me face to face
And this was hard for you to do
Because we were so much in love
And the times we shared were wonderful
But you felt something was missing
Because you're scared

As I fall into the chair in shock
I reach for the phone to call you
As it rings twice before you pick up
And you say hello as your voice cracks
As you start to cry on the phone
And tell me that you are sorry for this
Nevertheless, you do not want to make this hard
Because you think this is best for us both
And I try to talk you into coming home
Therefore, we can talk this out
But you say this is how it must be
And that I need to move on without you
Because you're scared

As you try to get off of the phone
I tell you I love you with all my heart
And you begin to cry profusely
As you think of the good times, we shared
But that is not enough to change your mind
Because you want to be, free
And I start to have an anxiety attack
As the tears, begin to run down my face
However, I cannot imagine what went wrong
Just because everything was fine as I left
And we were making some major plans
That we were preparing to complete
For our life long, journey together
But as you can see, things can change overnight
Because you're scared

The Scent of a Woman

The workweek is done and I need to relax
As I arrive home my phone rings
I go to answer it and it is my cousin
And he is ready to go out to the club
However, I am hesitant to go hang out
Because I really just want to chill
And he convinces me to hangout
As I go get ready for the club
He pulls up with his friends
And we head out to a surprise spot
But as we pay to enter the club
I hear this sensual voice walk by
As I scan through the crowd
To see the beauty attached to the voice
I come up empty on finding her
However, I smell the Scent of a Woman

As we head over to the table to sit down
And I walk over to the bar
To get a drink I hear her voice
As I turn to see the owner
I just miss her in the group of women that walk away
Nevertheless, I have an idea of where she may be
I head back to the table to tell my cousin
However, he and his friends are out on the dance floor
As I sip on my drink until they return
However, I cannot see her through the darkness
As I hear her, lovely voice getting closer
I get up to see if I can pick her out in the crowd
Nevertheless, all I could pick up was the Scent of a Woman

As I get back to the table to sit down
I see my cousin approaching me
And he tells me I have a secret admirer
However, he promised her he would not point her out
I would have to trust in my instincts
And that he would love to be in my shoes
Because he tells me that, she is a very attractive
As he goes on and on about her beauty
I hear that sensual voice say hello
As I turn around to see her up close
And her astounding beauty stuns me
Because I am speechless and at a loss for words
As I continue to look deep in her eyes
And smelling the lovely Scent of a Woman

Second to None

My mind is working overtime
Because all I can do is, think of you
And it keeps playing tricks with my heart
As the hours, pass me by
And the clock seems to be standing still
Because I just cannot shake this feeling
As it is weighing heavily on my soul
And my head keeps spinning
Just knowing that you are gone
And the pain that I have caused is second to none

You believed in me with all your heart
And I threw it all away for one night
Because I allowed myself to play
And it cost me your trust & love
As I know what it is, like to be a fool
Because I lost my heart & soul
And I cannot get back what we had
As I ripped out your heart
Because the pain is second to none

We meet for the very last time to talk
And I get down on my knees & beg
As I pray that, you can forgive me
But as I look into your eyes and see the pain
I know that nothing will change your mind
Because of what you feel inside your soul
As the tears, begin to flow down your face
And I tell you that, I am truly sorry
However, you cannot forget what I have done
Because it hurts you deep inside
And I know this is not a dream
Because the pain is second to none

Sexy & Sweet

Looking out upon a star
Wishing you were here
Therefore, I can hold you
And squeeze you tight
While I whisper in your ear
I Love U!
So you know how much
I need and want you
Because my love is strong
And you bring me joy
Because you're so Sexy & Sweet

Listen to my soul
While my heart
Calls out for you
And beats faster
When you are next to me
Because whatever you need
I will spend my life
Making all your dreams
And wishes come true
Because you're so Sexy & Sweet

I know you feel something
But you are scared & confused
That is fine with me
All I want to do
Is love you like?
You want to be loved
And I am hoping
You hire me for the job

Because I will travel
To the end of the earth
Just to love you
Caress you
Hold you
Kiss you
Squeeze you
And pamper you
Just like the queen you are
Because you're so Sexy & Sweet

Are you ready for love?
Just say yes
And your life can change forever
I promise many surprises
With no strings attached
I just want to be your man
And want you to be my lady
So what will it be?
Because no matter what
I will always love you
Because you're so Sexy & Sweet

Sexy Lover

I cannot shake the feelings that are in my head
But by having these feelings I want you more & more
We both cannot fight the temptations that we have inside
That is why you are my sexy lover

You can only imagine what is in store
However, I tell you this you will be asking for more
Starting with your sexy lips
And working my way inch by inch
To the tips of your sexy toes
What this may lead up too
Only our hearts will know
That is why you are my sexy lover

I know you want me to chill
However, your beauty keeps me going
And your smile turns me on
When I am around you, I lose control
However, I do know one thing
That is you are my sexy lover

I think I will end here
And let your mind fill in the rest
But don't worry its worth every thought
And it just feels right in my heart
About how I feel for you
Because I have never felt this way about anyone
That is all I will say right now
Just that you are my sexy lover

Sexy, Kind & Unforgettable

As I walk toward the terminal
And prepare to board the plane
I look back with tears in my eyes
As you stand at a distance
And you blow me a kiss
But I just cannot stop the tears
As they run fast down my face
And I shout I love you
Because you're sexy, kind & unforgettable

I reach my seat on the plane
And place my bags overhead
As I sit and stare out the window
I imagine you right next to me
But I know that we will be apart
And just knowing in my heart, you're missed
As the plane lifts, off into the darkness
I will keep you on my mind always
Because you're sexy, kind & unforgettable

I can't stop crying just knowing were apart
But I close my eyes and think of happy times
As I slowly drift, off into a light sleep
I picture us playing along the beach
Running around splashing water
And tackling each other in the sand
As I, scoop you up off your feet
And begin to carry you towards the beach house
Therefore, I do not have to walk back on my own
Because you're sexy, kind & unforgettable

As we reach the beach house, I put you down
And you place my face in your hands
As you move in close to give me a kiss
Because you are feeling some type of way
And I see the look in your eyes of joy
As you, caress me in your arms
I start to get emotional upon your chest
And I just cannot believe I'm here with you
Because you're sexy, kind & unforgettable

As you look down upon me
And tell me that you will never let go
As you, wipe away my tears
And this is where I want to be
Because there is something special inside of me
That makes your heart pour out love
And it drives you wild & crazy
As you, begin to touch my arm
I hear a voice and then I wake up
And notice it is the flight attendant on the plane
Telling me that we have landed
As I realize it was all a dream
However, it seemed so real and true
And I know that I miss you already
Because you're sexy, kind & unforgettable

Shoulder To Lean On!

When you need a friend
You can count on me
Nevertheless, I confide in one
When I need female advice
That is my sister Cheryl
Because I know, I can trust her advice
When it comes to my wellbeing
And she is an angel
When I need her the most
Just being you is special
When I need a shoulder to lean on

You always look out for me
And you told me about Kelly
However, I do not want to impose
On her life at a bad time
And make things complicated
Nevertheless, your judgment has been on point
Therefore, I cannot go wrong
With your words of confidence
When I need a shoulder to lean on

You can always believe in one
If you just open up
And talk to someone like Cheryl
Because if she doesn't have
The exact answer
She puts things in perspective
And makes you think

About what's going on inside
While she's also racking her brain
For the right solution
As you, need a shoulder to lean on!

The reason we see eye to eye
Is because we've been through a lot
In the past
To make us individually stronger
That is why we are so close
We understand one another
With our eyes closed
In the darkest places
That is what you call a friend
When you need a shoulder to lean on

I would like to end
This with some words of wisdom
Whatever you do, do not change
No matter what anyone says about you
Just to let you know
You have my respect and trust
And I am there if you need an ear
Or to talk about any situation
If I can help
And if you need a shoulder to lean on

Silent Wish

As I step out upon the porch
To get a breath of fresh air
The site I am witnessing is lovely
As the stars shine upon the ocean
And the evening breeze blows the sand
While the moonlight captures my soul
Just as I picture you standing here
Right next to me within my arms
As I whisper in your ear
And I feel the pain in my heart
Because I am thinking of a Silent Wish

As I snap out of my daydream
And come back to reality
Just knowing that you are not here
Is driving me up a wall
And my life seems lost without you
However, as they say things happen for a reason
And I know the pain that is in my heart
Is not going to mend for quite sometime
Because you are not going to comeback
And all I can do is call upon a Silent Wish

I sit here and reminisce of all the good times
And the laughs we shared together
But it gets harder each and everyday
As the time passes with us being apart
Because I know that, it is over forever
And I cannot stop thinking about you
Nevertheless, I see that you are moving on with your life
And it shows that it is finally over between us
However, I know no matter what I will love you always
And I can only hope for it to change
As I call upon a Silent Wish

Snuggle Blanket

I sit here looking at your picture
Wishing you were here with me
As I stare at your pretty smile
And those sexy soft lips
Along with that beautiful curly hair of yours
Makes my head go into a tailspin
And I cannot wait to see you
And hold you close to me
Because you're my snuggle blanket

We have good times when we are together
And you take away my pain
When we talk and your next to me
I cannot explain the joy I have with you
But it is something that I hope I never lose
Because you bring me, comfort
And security when you squeeze me tight
Because you're my snuggle blanket

I hate to see you upset or mad
Because it brings me, down
However, I always provide open arms
Therefore, if you need to cry I am here
And if you just want a hug & kiss
I will have them waiting for you
But no matter what your precious to me
And you have a protector in me
Because you're my snuggle blanket

I dream of taking walks in the park with you
And holding your hand as we watch the sunset
As we dance in the rain until we get cold
And go inside to dry off and sit by the fire
Until we get warm and cozy
But as dreams sometimes come true
And sometimes that can be reality
I still keep you on my mind
And in my thoughts
Because you're my snuggle blanket

Special

Words cannot express
How I feel about you
Because I don't think
There is any word
That can describe
What I feel for you
Because you're Special

You appeared in my life
At the right time
And it was wonderful
Because I fell in love
With you as a person
Not with your beauty
Or for your body
But for how sweet
And gentle you are inside
Because you're Special

I want you more & more
And it makes me sad
Because I know
It will not ever happen
Because you only
Have feelings for me
As a friend
And I wish for more
However, I value our friendship
Because you're Special

It is hard for me
To hold in my feelings
And not react on them
Because at times
I want to hold you close
And kiss you all over
As that just entices
My thoughts & feelings for you
Because you're Special

Only if your feelings
Were the same
Then you would see
What you mean to me
Because you're my world
And I want you as my queen
Therefore, I can pamper you
With everything from
Diamonds to pearls
Minks to furs
And many other deeds
Because you're Special

Stolen Moments

As I look upon the stars up above
I sit and wish that you were here
Because the scent of your cologne
Sends goose bumps up my spine
And I cannot get you out of my mind
I just want to be inside your arms
As the moonlight gazes off of our souls
But with you being away so much
I can't wait until you come back home
Because I am fighting these Stolen Moments

As I wake up to this cloudy Saturday morning
I realize that you are not lying next to me
But as I roll over onto your pillow
I get a whiff of your wonderful scent
As it makes my body quiver from head to toe
I close my eyes and image your gentle touch
As you move it up and down my body
While my temperature begins to rise
And my soul begins to lose control
Because I am fighting these Stolen Moments

As I walk to the kitchen to get some wine
And head back over to the couch
As I stare into the fireplace burning
And begin to look at our pictures together
I fade into my perfect fantasy world
Because I can't stop thinking about you & me

As we stroll down the coastline hand n hand
While the cool breeze takes my breath away
And I stare into those dark brown eyes
I just lose all control of my soul
Because I miss you so very much
And hope and pray that you arrive soon
Because I am fighting these Stolen Moments

As the rainstorm outside is crashing against the house
I finish off the wine bottle by the fireplace
And I curl up into a ball under the blanket
As I slowly faded into a light sleep
And I begin to dream of you holding me close
Because I feel so safe with your arms around me
I start feeling a tickle upon my neck
And I just swipe at the sensation upon my neck
As I turn toward the inside of the couch
I begin to hear a whisper in my ear
As I roll over toward the fireplace
My eyes begin to tear and my face lights up
It is my baby standing there in the flesh
As I jump up into his strong arms
Because I am done fighting these Stolen Moments

Stormy Weather

The lights are out all over town
And I cannot reach you on the phone
As I'm trying to get home to you
And make sure that you are safe
Because I want to be there to protect you
As the darkness in the town settles
I cannot get to you fast enough
Therefore, I can hold you close in my arms
Until the lights come back on
Through the stormy weather

I finally make it home and rush inside
To find you cuddled up in the chair sleep
And as I shine the flashlight on your face
It looks like you had been crying
And I see your cell phone in your hand
As I wake you up and you see, it is me
You jump up out of the chair
Into my arms and squeeze me tight
Because you tried to reach me on the phone
And you could not get through to me
Because the service lines were down
And you had placed in your mind bad thoughts
But as you were holding me tight
You realized that I made it to you safely
Through the stormy weather

As we walk toward the couch to sit down
You stop in front of the bookcase
And drop to your knees in prayer
As the tears roll down your face
I kneel down next to you
And place my loving arms around you
As I close my eyes to pray along
Because I am overjoyed to be right next to you
As the weather outside tried to stop me
From getting home to you safely
Through this stormy weather

As we finish praying and stand up
And we walk over to the couch
I begin to wipe away your tears
And move in close to give you a kiss
I have a flashback of my travels
To get home to you through this storm
And all I could think about is being next to you
Along with all of the great times we shared
And how happy I would be to see your smile
Because you mean the world to me
And I just prayed to make it to you safely
Through this stormy weather

Sweet Prince

As I walk toward the balcony
And slide the door open
I begin to stare out into space
Because I can't get you off my mind
And I wish you were here with me
As I know seeing, you will bring me joy
However, my job has kept us apart for months
And I cannot sleep at night
Because I want to hold you in my arms
And never ever let you go
Nevertheless, I cannot wait to see your beautiful face
Because I will shower you with kisses
As I cater to your every beckon call
Because you're my queen
And I am your sweet prince

As the days pass by and my nights are lonely
I just pray to see my baby soon
Because my heart is filled with sadness
And it feels as if I am going to die
However, just as the tears begin to fall
I get a call on the phone
As I rush to pick it up hoping it was you
Nevertheless, it was just the front desk of the hotel
Just asking me to come to the lobby
And as I grab my key to head down
I see my boss in the hallway
And he wants me to go have a drink
As soon as I'm done at the front desk

My mood for drinks change
As I approach the desk along with my boss
I see the hotel manager smiling from ear to ear
And I cannot even imagine what is going on
Just as I turn to ask my boss a question
I see my baby standing by his side
As I drop to my knees in shock
Because my prayers have been answered
And I can hold my queen in my arms
As she receives kisses from her sweet prince

Tasty Love

We have our differences but I love you
And just when you have your doubts
Just remember our first kiss
Because it meant the world to me
As my soul began to quiver inside
And it made my heart skip a beat
But that made it that much more sweeter
Because I knew at that point you were the one
And I had finally found my tasty love

What we have is a unique blessing
Because you walked into my life
As my blue skies were dark
And the light at the end of my tunnel was dim
Your smile brought my sunshine back
And it eased the pain in my soul
But just as you think things are bad
God always provides you salvation
And mine was my sweet tasty love

Time For Love Is Up!

We all have dreams to be loved
But finding that love is hard
And it could never happen
So take risk to find out
Because you can pass up
The best thing ever
And miss happiness
Just ask me
Because I lust to be loved
By someone that will love me
The way I can love them
However, my ship may have passed
And I can only wonder
If my time for love is up

I bare my soul to women
And I am always being stepped upon
But the footprints never fade
Because of the pain
And I just pour out tears
Until my eyes
Can't cry no more tears
And I fade into the dark
Just wondering over & over
If my time for love is up

How much pain can a soul take?
Because you only can endure
So much pain
Before you shut down
And go crazy
In your mind, body & soul
And when that happens
You lose yourself in darkness
And it makes me wonder
If my time for love is up

I sit alone at night
Just praying to be saved
From the constant pain
I feel inside
And wish for the best
But I get pulled deeper
Into the darkness
By the sorrow
That I feel inside
While I fade deep
Into the darkness
I just keep wondering
If my time for love is up

If past relationships, indicate
How it is going to be
I do not stand a chance
To be happy or to be loved
Because the statement
Of nice guys finish last
Holds true each day
And it tears me apart
Because all of the failures
That I have encountered
Over my lifetime
And this is why I wonder
If my time for love is up

Being the only child is tough
Because you don't have
That brother or sister
To turn to and rely on
Which makes it difficult?
Because you feel lost
And can't find that strength
To survive and pull through
Just hoping to be saved
By that true love
You have craved for
Makes me wonder
If my time for love is up

True Friend

I thought the world of you
And let you into my heart
By telling you my secrets
And sharing my feelings
Because I fell for you
And what we had was special
But after the cold shoulder
And the distance between us
Just proved to me
You were never a True Friend!

Girl, you made me look foolish
Because I trusted you
And all I got was this added pain
Nevertheless, I cannot get you off my mind
Just hoping that it's all a dream
However, as the days go by
I know it is for real
And my heart aches
Because of the way you have been acting
Just remember one thing
You were never a True Friend!

Life is full of surprises
Because you always look for love
And when you think you have found it
With that, perfect someone
And everything tends to line-up
Until reality sets in
Then she drops the bomb
By just not talking to you
And you do not even know why
However, that just proves
You were never a True Friend!

True friends stay to the end
No matter how bad things get
And they respect each other
Because what they have is special
But when one of you
Just stops the communication
It proves that your friendship
Was just a big lie
And just proves to me
You were never a True Friend!

Uncertain

Life bring trials and tribulations
And I am trying to stay afloat
But it becomes harder each & everyday
Because as I stand up I get knocked down
And it takes its toll on my soul
Nevertheless, I just have to carry on
And withstand the pain
Because my life is uncertain

I pray to survive every day & night
As it seems to get harder day after day
However, I have to be strong for my kids
And for them to see me hurting is not an option
Nevertheless, with them in my corner, it makes me strong
As I keep wondering about my wellbeing
Because my life is uncertain

I want that special someone in my life
That will bring me happiness and joy
However, I keep settling for less than I deserve
And I need to step back and observe my heart
Because for me & my kids we deserve the best
And if I never find that true love
I will be ok with that no matter what
Because I will always have my kids
And they will never let me be lonely
Because they will always be by my side
And love me forever each day
While my life may seem uncertain

Void in My Heart

As I sit here while my heart is crying
And I do not understand these feelings
Because I am yearning for you
And just knowing you are moving on
Has finally settled in my mind
And it is tearing me up inside
However, I have no one to blame except me
Because I chose to let you go
And now that you are finding happiness
I am feeling the void in my heart

I talked with you on the phone
And the sound of your voice was sweet
As it brought back memories
And it seemed you were right next to me
Because I closed my eyes to dream of you
And I smelled the scent of your perfume
As I reached out to pull you, close
Therefore, I could hold you tight in my arms
You began to fade away in my dream
And at that, moment is when it hit me
There is a void in my heart

I do not know if I made the right decision
Nevertheless, all my life I have made bad choices
And this time was no different in my life
Because I may have thrown away true love
That is something that is hard to find
But I am wishing you'd found happiness
As I know when our time ran out
It was not just hard on you & him
However, I am hurting inside pretty bad
And I just did not know what to do
Nevertheless, I am hurting for other reasons now
And that is because of the void in my heart

Walk Away

I do not know what is wrong with us
Nevertheless, I try to get answers from you
And you will not return my calls
As time goes by it is obvious to me
That your feelings have changed for me
And if that is true do not string me along
Because I cannot take the pain
However, if that is what you want from me
All you have to do is say the word
And I will just walk away

I know times are rough being in love
However, that comes with the territory
And when the rough get going
That does not mean you have to run
Because no relationship is perfect
Overall, I still love you
And if that has changed for you
Please be upfront and tell me
Therefore, I can give you what you want
That is to be free from me
And I will walk away

You told me you needed time to think
And I gave you your space that you wanted
As the hours and the days passed
I have not heard from you
And I hope everything is ok
However, I will let you reach out to me
Because you will know, where we stand
And if you decide that, you need to be free
I will grant you your wish
But believe me it will be painful
And I will not stand in your way
But all I can say is I wish you well
As I kiss you for the last time
And begin to walk away

Warmed My Soul

It was a hot summer night
And I was sitting here all alone
Trying to wipe away my pain
That I have deep inside my soul
And just as I glanced up you walk by
With your lovely dark brown hair
And that silky brown skin
As you had heads turning left & right
I thought I was looking at an angel
Therefore, I had to pinch myself
To make sure I was not dreaming
Because your beauty warmed my soul

As you looked down at me and smiled
I almost fell out of my chair
As you turned and waved at me
I gathered myself and waved back
And I started to make my way toward you
As I began to get closer and closer
My knees began to get weak
And my hands started to tremble
Because your beauty warmed my soul

We began to talk to one another
And I could not get over your smile
It just brightened the room
And it caused me to be hypnotized
As my soul began to lose control
With each and every moment
Because your beauty warmed my soul

As we talked for hours to get acquainted
You begin to stare out onto the dance floor
And as you turn around, I ask you to dance
But you're hesitate at first to say yes
Because you don't like the song
However, you accept my offer anyway
And just as we begin to dance
To the song "The Sweetest Love"
You place your arms around my neck
As you start to sing along to the music
Nevertheless, I cannot get past your beauty
Because with each word of the song
I fall deeper and deeper for you
Because your beauty warms my soul

When Our Eyes Met

Standing across the room
I noticed a lovely queen
As I moved through the crowd
To get closer to her standing there
She walked outside to get some air
And I knew that this could not be a dream
Because her beauty captured my attention
And her smile was like a ray of sunshine
But as she entered the club again
And she looked up toward me
That is when our eyes met

As the club stood still
Just for that split second
And our hearts skipped a beat
Because I could not believe, it was her
A classmate from high school
And we have not seen each other in years
But as she called out my name
And reached out to give me a hug
I was in shock of her radiant beauty
Even more now after all these years
And telling her she was sexy
Would not really do her any justice
Because that is when our eyes met

Within Your Hearts

Baby, life is too short
To let the one you love
Just get up and walk away
You must make an effort
To hold onto that special someone
Before that, someone is gone
Because when that love is gone
You will not know how much
He or she means to you
Until they are really gone
So you must pray to God
And hope there is a soft spot
In their heart to give a second chance
At the love you still hold
Within your hearts

When the opportunity is near
Take your step forward
And do not turn back
Because with a blink of an eye
You might not ever get the chance
To make the situation clear
And be happy again
So do not hesitate to act
When you know what you want
And your love is still
Within your hearts

Work Family

In Loving Memory of Sarah M. Richardson
Being a part of this shift
Is an honor to me?
Because without each one of you
There would be no me
Although we might have our disagreements
We still learn to beat the odds
And come together as a team
I would just thank you all
For putting up with me
And just being my family away from home
May God bless every one of you?
Through our travels together
In the near future
And may we keep up the hard work
As we enter each New Year
With our minds focused
And our heads up high
I wish we could all stay together as a team forever
However, I know all good things ends

This is coming from the heart of all of your work family!

Thank you for making the work place a happy one
And being a part of my work family as well!

Yearn For You

It is late and I cannot sleep
I get up out of bed
And head downstairs
As you run through my mind
And I wish you were near
Being apart so long
Drives me up a wall
And I think of what
I want to do to you
But just knowing you're away
I yearn for you!

Today is the day
And my baby will be home
Because I miss her
From head to toe and can't wait
To show her how much I missed you
I have things mapped out
First, I will carry you in from outside
And bring you a glass of wine
Tell you to relax
Because tonight's the night
I yearn for you!

I hear your car pull up
And I meet you at the door
Tell you to wait there
As I take your bags inside
And comeback to give you a kiss & a hug
As I sweep you off your feet
And carry you to the couch

As I place you, down gently
Because your smile makes me
Yearn for you!

You look at the table spread
And you know now
That I am going to be naughty
With the strawberries & whip cream
And the flavored edible oils
As I remove your shoes
And start to massage your feet
Then work my way to your thighs
And then to your juicy breast
Just watching you squirm
I begin to yearn for you!

You want to go get changed
And go slip into something comfortable
As you, tell me to close my eyes
Because you have a surprise
And for me just wait and see
As I sit and wait
I smell your sweet scent
As you, get closer
I begin to yearn for you!

As you, touch my face
And tell me to open my eyes
I am at a loss for words
And my jaw drops
As you, model your new nightgown
I grab a drink to regain my composure
Because your see through night gown
Just blows my mind
As I yearn for you!

As I catch my breathe
And you move closer
My heart skips a beat
As I brace for your
Sensitive touch upon my skin
I pull you close
Therefore, I can caress your body
As I feed you strawberries
I yearn for you!

As I remove your gown
And lay your head upon the pillow
As rub you down with oils
And cover you from head to toe
While I start at your lips
And work my way down
To your neck
And then your breast
On down to your belly button
And bypassing your center

As I stop at your thighs
And work my way to your feet
As I kiss each toe separately
Because now you know
I yearn for you!

As you scratch and moan
I think it is time to set you off right
As I spread your legs
And work my way
To your private place
And grab some ice
To lick you up & down

And around & around
As you, push me in deeper
And yell out my name
Because I yearn for you

Now the mood is set
And we start to make love
As I stroke you up and down
You dig your nails into my back
And I do not want you to stop
Because I have fallen
In love with you all over again
As our bodies, begin to sweat
And our collective juices
Start to heat up along with the passion
As I yearn for you!

You look into my eyes
And do not have to say a word
Because what you're thinking
Has touched my soul
With your love and joy
You have given to me
And I am thankful you are in my life
As our passionate night
Comes to an end
Nevertheless, just so you know
I Love you the same now
As I did when we first met
Because I still yearn for you!

www.ingramcontent.com/pod-product-compliance
Lightning Source LLC
LaVergne TN
LVHW041803060526
838201LV00046B/1105